A Month of Prayer & Gratitude

A Month of Prayer & Gratitude

Five-Minute Meditations for a Deeper Experience of Gratitude

Includes Daily Prayers by Leo S. Thorne

Edited by W. Douglas Hood Jr. *and* Leo S. Thorne

Foreword by Susan Sparks

WIPF & STOCK · Eugene, Oregon

A MONTH OF PRAYER AND GRATITUDE
Five-Minute Meditations for a Deeper Experience of Gratitude

Copyright © 2024 Wipf and Stock Publishers. All rights reserved. Except for brief quotations in critical publications or reviews, no part of this book may be reproduced in any manner without prior written permission from the publisher. Write: Permissions, Wipf and Stock Publishers, 199 W. 8th Ave., Suite 3, Eugene, OR 97401.

Wipf & Stock
An Imprint of Wipf and Stock Publishers
199 W. 8th Ave., Suite 3
Eugene, OR 97401

www.wipfandstock.com

PAPERBACK ISBN: 979-8-3852-3608-4
HARDCOVER ISBN: 979-8-3852-3609-1
EBOOK ISBN: 979-8-3852-3610-7

VERSION NUMBER 12/23/24

All Scripture quotations, unless noted otherwise, are taken from the Common English Bible, copyright © 2011. Used by permission. All rights reserved.

Scripture quotations marked (KJV) are from the King James or Authorized Version.

Scripture quotations marked (NIV) are taken from the Holy Bible, New International Version®, NIV®. Copyright © 1973, 1978, 1984, 2011 by Biblica, Inc.™ Used by permission of Zondervan. All rights reserved worldwide. www.zondervan.com The "NIV" and "New International Version" are trademarks registered in the United States Patent and Trademark Office by Biblica, Inc.™

Scripture quotations marked (NRSV) are from the New Revised Standard Version Bible, © 1989, by the Division of Christian Education of the National Council of the Churches of Christ in the U.S.A. Used by permission. All rights reserved.

Scripture quotations marked (NRSVue) are taken from the New Revised Standard Version Updated Edition. Copyright © 2021 National Council of Churches of Christ in the United States of America. Used by permission. All rights reserved worldwide.

Contents

Foreword by Susan Sparks | vii
Introduction | xi
Acknowledgments | xix
Contributors | xxiii
Abbreviations | xxvi

1 Gratitude Begins with God (Doug Hood) | 1
2 Meet Me at Ten Minutes to Seven in Your Heart (Thomas K. Tewell) | 4
3 An Attitude of Gratitude (Michael B. Brown) | 8
4 Foundations (Doug Hood) | 11
5 Praying Like a Child (Nathanael Hood) | 14
6 Sarah's Purse (Susan Sparks) | 17
7 A Thankful People (Doug Hood) | 20
8 Never Too Many Stamps (Bruce Main) | 23
9 Borrowing Time for Prayer (Doug Hood) | 25
10 Profit, Loss, and Gratitude (Nathanael Hood) | 28
11 Work in Progress (Greg Rapier) | 31
12 The Christian Way of Life (Doug Hood) | 34
13 What Group Are We? (Grace Cameron Hood) | 37
14 Jealousy, the Enemy of Gratitude (Nathanael Hood) | 40
15 When It Is Hard to Pray (Doug Hood) | 43
16 Life's Undertow (Yvonne Martinez Thorne) | 46

Contents

17 Summons to Gratitude (Doug Hood) | 49
18 Praying New York–Style (Bruce Main) | 52
19 Write Them on Your Doorframes (Nathanael Hood) | 54
20 God's Apparent Inattention to Prayer (Doug Hood) | 57
21 Mark Twain's Favorite Word (Thomas K. Tewell) | 60
22 Thanksgiving in Bonaire (Doug Hood) | 63
23 More than Conquerors (Yvonne Martinez Thorne) | 66
24 When You Don't Know How to Pray (Doug Hood) | 69
25 It's Still Life (Susan Sparks) | 72
26 Quiet, Lonely Places (Nathanael Hood) | 75
27 Conditions of Answered Prayers (Doug Hood) | 78
28 Wheat and Weeds (Michael B. Brown) | 81
29 God's Treasures (Grace Cameron Hood) | 84
30 Two Little Words (Nathanael Hood) | 87
31 Beyond the Fence (Greg Rapier) | 90

Sermons
An Attitude of Gratitude (Michael B. Brown) | 92
Am I Gonna Ride This Thing or Not? (Susan Sparks) | 100
FOMO (Thomas K. Tewell) | 107
Secret of Contentment (Bruce Main) | 116
Gratitude (Hannah Anglemyer) | 120

Bibliography | 123

Foreword

Held Together by the Grace of God

SUSAN SPARKS

> And all things are held together in him.—Colossians 1:17b

One Christmas during the height of COVID-19, I wrote a sermon using the metaphor of a tiny Christmas cactus that had just bloomed on our windowsill—a sign of life in the darkest days of December. To illustrate the sermon, I planned to show the little plant on the live stream. But as the old saying goes, we plan, and God laughs.

The day I was to record the sermon, I walked into the church holding the tiny cactus like a newborn baby bird, its bright pink bloom dangling precariously off one of its branches. Placing the cactus just out of view of the camera, I hit record. I was only a few words in when, suddenly, the little pink blossom detached itself from the cactus branch and dropped to the carpet. I hit pause on the camera and stared down at the pink dot. My entire sermon was lying on the floor. The only thing I knew to do was pray: "Dear Lord in heaven, please make that blossom fly up and reattach itself." The Lord heard my prayer, for when I opened my eyes, I spied the Scotch tape. Quickly taping the blossom back on the cactus, I hit record and finished the sermon.

FOREWORD

Some days, we're all just trying to hold it together by any means possible. And many days, like that little blossom, we feel like we just can't hang on. The grace of God is all we have left.

This wonderful book you are holding, *A Month of Prayer and Gratitude*, provides a lifeline to that grace. My dear friends, Rev. Drs. W. Douglas Hood Jr. and Leo S. Thorne (who is also my colleague from the American Baptist Churches USA), have created this beautiful collection of meditations and prayers that act as "holy tape" to help us hold on.

The ancient monastics taught a fundamental rhythm for the balancing and ordering of human life. It was called prayer and praxis—or prayer and work. Prayer (along with gratitude, its core element) connects us to the holy and transforming power of God, which, in turn, gives us the power to "hang on" and continue the work we were put here to do. This book calls us into this holy rhythm.

Each day, the book offers a starting Scripture, then moves to a short meditation from Doug (and others) about incorporating prayer and gratitude into our daily lives. The wonderfully diverse and creative messages offer hope and new ways to reframe how we experience difficulties such as change, grief, jealousy, loss, cynicism, rage, and despair—things that can drain us of our strength and make us question whether we can go on. The profound sense of faith, truth, and lived experience that Doug brings to these messages reaches deep into the human heart and holds us tight.

After each meditation comes a word of prayer from Leo. His prayers will make you feel not just connected but duct-taped to the Spirit. Okay, yes, I'm a fellow Baptist, and I may be a bit biased, but as you begin to read, you will feel the power of his prayers and a blossoming of hope that we might—just might—be able to hang on.

Several weeks after my sermon blossom disaster, I noticed the tiniest stain of pink on the end of another branch of my Christmas cactus. That little plant was going to try again.

Foreword

Sometimes, you have to Scotch-tape things together until hope peeks back out. And it always does. In the meantime, hold it together with Doug and Leo, and the grace of God will do the rest.

Introduction

"All life is just a progression toward, and then a recession from, one phrase—'I love you,'" F. Scott Fitzgerald wrote.[1] Prayer is a progression toward God; the nearer one draws to God, the more palpable it becomes that God is love. One verse in 1 John sparkles on this subject: "God is love, and those who remain in love remain in God and God remains in them" (1 John 4:16b). The progression toward God changes the character of one's prayers. Early in one's progression, prayers are shaped by self-desire. God is asked to grant what we have determined to be best for us. As one's progression draws closer to God, the brilliance, clarity, and power of God's love become sufficient for all needs and wants. As Harry Emerson Fosdick once cited a prayer from northern India, "O Lord, we know not what is good for us. Thou knowest what it is. For it we pray."[2]

Along the progression of prayer, several discoveries come into focus. First, prayer deepens our relationship with God. Words are inadequate for speaking of the relationship, much as they are with any relationship. Rather, the relationship must be experienced. A rare opportunity presented itself some years ago that provided clarity on this matter. My wife, Grace; my colleague in ministry, Elisabeth Wilson; and I were invited as guests in the studio during the taping of an episode of *Good Morning America*. We were not guests on the show. We were guests of the *GMA*

---

1. Fitzgerald, "Offshore Pirate," 83.
2. Buttrick, *Christian Fact*, 191.

INTRODUCTION

hosts, invited to stand among the camera crew during the show's taping. Among the special guests on the holiday episode that morning was the chef Emeril Lagasse. Sam Champion, weatherman for the morning show, suddenly thought it would be a good idea to personally introduce me to Mr. Lagasse.

Mr. Champion asked me to accompany him downstairs to the ABC studio. Emeril Lagasse was demonstrating for *GMA*'s audience the preparation of a holiday dessert. At the conclusion of the demonstration, Lagasse invited Champion to "taste" the completed dessert. Sam Champion did, and the look on Champion's face pleased Lagasse. What happened next was unexpected—evidenced by the producer and camera crew's confusion. Champion grasped another fork, cut again into the dessert, and held it to my mouth. "Doug, you must taste this!" Champion insisted. The studio cameras continued to shoot for all of America to see this moment of spontaneity. I had two choices. I could demand that Champion prove to me that the dessert was as good as he claimed before I opened my mouth, or I could simply "taste" and see for myself. Studio cameras rolling, I naturally opened my mouth. I agreed with Champion's assessment. Agreement didn't follow convincing proof. It followed an experience. Relationships are experienced.

That leads to the second discovery: prayer releases God's power in our lives. The apostle Paul writes the church in Philippi, "I can endure all these things through the power of the one who gives me strength" (Philippians 4:13). Paul is a prisoner in Rome. In a life dedicated to serving Christ, Paul has endured much—shipwreck, ridicule, hunger, and excruciating poverty. Now, he sits in a Roman prison and writes that whatever the circumstances, he has learned the secret of inner strength and contentment. Perhaps even more remarkable, Paul lays aside his own needs and concerns to write a deeply personal letter to the Philippians to encourage them in their faith. Despite his imprisonment and impending trial, Paul's one desire is to share with the church in Philippi that joy and strength do not come from outward circumstances but from an intimate relationship with Jesus. That power is so tremendous and so available that Paul feels he can face anything, knowing that

Introduction

nothing can diminish his spirit. His spirit was invulnerable. Paul wants the Philippians to utilize that same power.

The interesting thing about the New Testament is that we find that same power animating most of the early Christians. A profession of faith in Jesus usually pushed people to the margins of their communities. Families were torn apart—mothers and daughters, fathers and sons, no longer in relationship with one another because one or the other had decided to become a follower of Jesus. Worship services were conducted in secret and often disrupted by Jewish leaders eager to destroy the Jesus movement. The worst tortures that could be imagined were invented and performed to discourage participation in the new Christian faith. There was every reason for ignoring the swelling growth of the Christian church, keeping one's head down, and simply avoiding trouble. Yet, for all the compelling reasons to remain separate from those following Jesus, men and women who believed in him made one dominating impression wherever they went: the impression of uncommon power.

That power has not been withdrawn. It is not a closely guarded secret. Where men and women continue to take Christ's attitude of loving others and serving others, that same power is unmistakable. What is troubling is that few would say that the church today impresses the world with the same power as it once did. Somehow, those who claim discipleship to Jesus Christ show little evidence of a changed life, a life of uncommon power. Absent in many Christians today is a sense of adequacy for meeting challenges and adversity. The membership and attendance decline of the Christian church has been tracked and documented for many years now. This has resulted in the publication of resources to perfect the church's hospitality, increase the vitality of its worship, and harness the power of technology. However valuable these may be, the most urgent need is for Christians to get back to that power that is possessed by the daily nurture of a personal fellowship with Jesus—a relationship that is deepened by prayer.

Return for a moment to the first two words of Paul in Philippians 4:13, "I can." Some years ago, I was working with a personal trainer named Michael Bishop. One day, he had me on my back, bench-pressing what seemed to be an incredible weight for me. After pushing the bar above my head several times, I did a controlled drop of the bar to my chest. I was depleted. I delivered an eye message to him to remove the bar from my chest. I will never forget his response, "That's not my bar. You place it back on the upright supports." Then, he did what his training taught him to do. He placed his hands around the bar with my own. That was simply to ensure that I didn't hurt myself. But the lifting belonged to me. I pushed with everything in me; I summoned all the power I could to lift the bar back onto the supports. As my strength began to fail, he matched the loss of my strength with his own until the bar had returned to rest on the support. Paul writes, "I can, through the power who gives me strength" (paraphrase of Philippians 4:13). If you are depressed or in trouble, say, "I can in him," and you will find God's strength come alongside your own. If you struggle with passions or addictions that frighten you, or if you feel that you are losing your grip on life, say, "I can in him," and you will discover an unseen hand on the bar with your own, matching and exceeding your own strength. The Christian's strength begins with "I can."

The third discovery in the progression of prayer is a state of gratitude. "Pastoral care's primary aim is to help people meet the true and living God when they experience profound disruption," writes Philip Browning Helsel.[3] Notice what is missing from that purpose statement—absent is any responsibility by the caregiver to "fix" or "heal" the one receiving care. The primary aim is to help people "meet the true and living God." That is enough. When God's presence is experienced by the wounded, the disillusioned, and the distressed, a soothing, comforting dynamic is present, much as that experienced by a child when a parent draws near. As James S. Stewart so wisely and imaginably observes, "For the whole life and power of the invisible God are standing beside you at this moment, to penetrate and transform any situation."[4] An experiential understanding

---

3. Helsel, *Pastoral Care and Counseling*, 40.
4. Stewart, *Walking with God*, 59.

INTRODUCTION

of God's presence helps suffering people make it through challenging times. That experience results in gratitude.

Some years ago, a difficult and unpopular decision was made by the governing board of the church I served as pastor. The decision disrupted the ministry of several engaged members of the church who had previously been serving with energy, enthusiasm, and joy. In their woundedness, they asked me to choose sides—do I stand with them or the governing board? I felt deeply their disappointment and hurt, but I felt the governing board had made the right decision. Shortly after the decision had been made, the truth of an old axiom, "wounded people wound others," was proven. When I sought to stand with them in their hurt, they publicly walked away from me, leaving me to stand alone. Laura Cooney, my administrative assistant, immediately saw what was happening and stepped up to stand by my side. No words were spoken by either of us. She simply stood alongside me in a difficult moment in the life of the church. I never imagined that something so simple could be so profound. That one demonstration of love and presence by Laura transformed the moment, changed my day, and continues to empower my ministry over a decade later. The chambers of my soul were filled with strength. Only the word "gratitude" is adequate, as I remember what Laura did for me.

My experience was shared by the apostle Paul. On three occasions, Paul approached God in prayer asking that some malady or difficulty be removed. The difficulty is not identified. Nor is it important. Each of us knows the challenge or pain of some illness, difficulty, or trial in life. Our prayer may be the same as Paul's, "Please, Lord, remove this from me." Yet, God's answer was no. What God did offer was God's presence, love, and strength. It was enough for Paul, and Paul expressed gratitude. On the night that Jesus was betrayed and handed over to the Roman guard, Jesus prayed, asking God to deliver him from what lay ahead. The humanity of Jesus was never more clearly seen than when he battled his fear of the crucifixion that faced him. God's answer was no. But God did send an angel to be with Jesus, and Jesus was strengthened (Luke 22:43). In each story, circumstances were not

INTRODUCTION

changed. Nor was my story changed by Laura standing with me. What was different is that fear and weakness were transformed into strength and courage. Prayer properly understood and practiced leads to one transforming experience, an invasion of supernatural strength from another place. From this, gratitude follows as naturally as our next breath.

This book is a follow-up to *A Month of Prayer: Five-Minute Meditations for a Deeper Experience of Prayer*. What has been curated here are daily meditations and sermons on prayer and gratitude by many distinguished preachers who have filled the pulpit of First Presbyterian Church of Delray Beach in the past twelve years. Also present are meditations by myself and Dr. Greg Rapier, my co-pastor of First Presbyterian Church; my son, Nathanael Hood, who has followed his own call into ministry; Dr. Yvonne Thorne, a resident American Baptist pastor in this congregation; Grace Cameron Hood, the director of Children and Family Ministry of First Presbyterian Church; and Hannah Anglemyer, a member of the church who delivered her included sermon on Youth Sunday, 2024. As with the first volume, *A Month of Prayer*, this volume is significantly stronger by the gifts of my co-editor, Dr. Leo S. Thorne. Leo has read and prayed over each meditation, opening his heart and mind to God for direction in the daily prayers that he crafted for each. Nearly a thousand copies of the first volume have been sold, and numerous readers continue to comment that the primary strength of that volume was Leo's prayers that seem to capture, with considerable clarity, their own heart's desires. I remain confident the same experience will be had by the readers of this volume.

As I wrote in the first volume, the most helpful practice of reading this book is to identify a time of day when you might spend a minimum of ten minutes alone with it and God. Five minutes will be for reading a single meditation along with its prayer of the day, and five minutes will be for stillness, reflecting upon what God may be saying to you through the words you've read. Try praying, "God, what would you have me hear?" and "What would you have me do?" The reader will benefit from reading this book as it is designed: one

INTRODUCTION

meditation a day for thirty-one days. Plowing through the book in one or two sittings will only diminish the value of any one of them. *A Month of Prayer and Gratitude* is not a book to be read as it is a collection of daily meditations that cultivate, slowly and over time, a deeper experience of gratitude.

With this collection of meditations and prayers, Leo and I hope to provide a pathway to a deeper experience of prayer and gratitude. A serious and passionate pursuit of prayer opens new experiences of gratitude. Exploring more deeply the experience of gratitude increases the discipline and power of prayer. A symbiotic relationship between the two is realized, drawing the reader into the wisdom of F. Scott Fitzgerald, "All life is just a progression toward, and then a recession from one phrase—'I love you.'" Loving God, and experiencing God's love, is central to human experience. A progression toward God in prayer and gratitude opens such a genuine and vital relationship.

Acknowledgments

Thomas Carlyle says that the ultimate question posed by life is this: "Wilt thou be a hero or a coward?"[1] Nearly thirty-eight years of ministry suggest to me that how we might answer this question depends, at the minimum, on the company we have chosen to keep. Just as there are people whose life orientation is failure to accept personal responsibility and to view life as unfair, there are others who have an inexhaustible stream of hope that flows through their life; a stream that maintains optimism and expectation even in the most challenging of circumstances. The primary difference, I contend, is the people whom they have kept company with, either in personal relationships or through the written word. My own personal life and my professional practice of ministry have received strength upon strength from the company I have kept, many of whom have accepted my invitation to contribute to this volume of meditations and sermons. I am grateful to every contributor to this book for how my life and ministry have been upheld, carried at times, and continually strengthened by their love, counsel, and participation in my ministry. Each voice collected in this volume has participated in my ministry here at First Presbyterian Church of Delray Beach over these nearly thirteen years. I remain grateful to each one of them as I now anticipate my retirement. It is my immeasurable joy to share them again with this community of faith through these pages.

1. Bonnell, *No Escape from Life*, 6.

Acknowledgments

Keep company with each of them, read their work on these pages again and again, and your life will be lived as a hero.

Leo Thorne and I continue to be astonished by the capacity of Nancy Fine, the business administrator of the church, to take the written words of this volume, read them carefully, correcting mistakes in spelling and tense along the way, verifying the accuracy of the endnotes, and preparing the manuscript to the exacting standards of the publisher. Quite simply, we are grateful for everything that happened in Nancy's care once words were placed on paper that made the publication of this volume possible.

The music ministry of this church, under the leadership of Don Cannarozzi and Birgit Djupedal Fioravante, has been described frequently by guests in worship as a wonder. The consistent excellence of music, week after week, is equal to any performance that may be enjoyed at the Broward Center for the Performing Arts—and frequently, members of our choir are featured performers at the Broward Center and other such venues! Often, the question is asked of clergy, who have the responsibility of preparing and leading worship: How do they experience worship for themselves? Not one Sunday in nearly thirteen years has that ever been a difficulty for preachers who preach here. The choir lifts the pastors, just as they do for the people who worship, into a sacred and holy place each week where God's presence and power become palpable. This book is dedicated to each of them with gratitude: Mario Arevalo, Marsha Bird, Oleksandr Donskyi, Julia Duca, Dan Dykstra, Devin Dykstra, Fernando Gonzalez, Penny Johnson, Robyn Lamp, Laura León, Neil Nelson, Shanna Nolan, Sharon O'Connor, Kyaunnee Richardson, Kathleen Shelton, and Alejandro Viera.

Leo and I especially want to acknowledge our spouses, Grace Cameron Hood and Dr. Yvonne Martinez Thorne, both of whose own work appears in these pages, for how their own close walk with our Lord strengthens our faith and practice of ministry. The blessings we have received from them are too numerous to count, and our lives are the richer for them. Perhaps the greatest blessing we continually receive from each of them is their ability to gently remind us of what our most important vocation is.

Acknowledgments

To you, the reader of this book, I am grateful that you have chosen to be intentional in your walk with our Lord by pursuing the collected wisdom and guidance found on these pages. Perhaps, by God's grace, this modest collection of meditations and sermons will inspire and strengthen you as you grow in prayer and gratitude. As David H. C. Read once spoke from the Madison Avenue Presbyterian Church pulpit in the city of New York, "It was the thankful response of the humble and the contrite that led Jesus to his own outburst of gratitude to God."[2]

---

2. Read, *Preacher*, 53.

Contributors

Hannah Anglemyer is a high school student in Palm Beach County, Florida. She is a third-generation member of the First Presbyterian Church of Delray Beach (PCUSA).

Rev. Dr. Michael B. Brown is the pastor at Blowing Rock Methodist Church (United Methodist) in North Carolina and a professor at Wake Forest University. He was previously the senior minister at Marble Collegiate Church (Reformed Church of America and the United Church of Christ) in New York City. He is an accomplished author, preacher, and teacher. He is married to Page, has four grown children, and resides in Winston-Salem, North Carolina.

Grace Cameron Hood is the director of Children and Family Ministry at First Presbyterian Church of Delray Beach (PCUSA). Grace has a BCE from Belhaven College and attended Columbia Theological Seminary. She is married to Doug, has two grown children, and resides in Boynton Beach, Florida.

Nathanael Hood has an MA from New York University, Tish, and an MDiv from Princeton Theological Seminary. He recently completed his chaplain residency and is seeking his first call. He is the son of Doug and Grace Hood and resides in New York City.

Rev. Dr. W. Douglas Hood Jr. is the co-pastor of the First Presbyterian Church of Delray Beach (PCUSA), Florida, where he has been on staff since 2012. He holds an MDiv from Columbia Theological Seminary and a DMin from Fuller Theological Seminary.

Contributors

An accomplished author, he is married to Grace, has two grown children, and resides in Boynton Beach, Florida.

Rev. Dr. Bruce Main has an MTh from Fuller Theological Seminary and a DMin from Princeton Theological Seminary. He is the founder and president of UrbanPromise in Camden, New Jersey, which has thirty-plus affiliate locations worldwide. He is married to Pamela, has three grown children, and resides in Haddonfield, New Jersey.

Rev. Dr. Greg Rapier is the co-pastor of the First Presbyterian Church of Delray Beach (PCUSA), Florida, where he has been on staff since 2018. He holds an MDiv from Princeton Theological Seminary and a DMin from Pittsburgh Theological Seminary. His writings have appeared in numerous publications. He is married to Lissette, has a son, and resides in Lake Worth, Florida.

Rev. Susan Sparks is the senior minister at Madison Avenue Baptist Church (American Baptist) in New York City. She received her BA at the University of North Carolina, a law degree from Wake Forest University, and an MDiv from Union Theological Seminary. A North Carolina native, she has been featured in *O Magazine*, the *New York Times*, and several television networks. She is married to Toby and resides in New York City.

Rev. Dr. Thomas K. Tewell is the founder of the Macedonian Ministry Foundation in Powder Springs, Georgia. Throughout his career, he served numerous pastorates, including Fifth Avenue Presbyterian Church (PCUSA) in New York City. An accomplished speaker and writer, he is married to Suzanne, has two grown sons, and resides in Claremont, California.

Rev. Dr. Leo S. Thorne is a retired associate general secretary for mission resource development for the American Baptist Churches USA. He has two master's degrees, including an MDiv from Drew University, a doctorate in American literature from Columbia Pacific University, and an honorary doctorate from the American Baptist Seminary of the West. A retired senior pastor, university English professor, and senior university administrator, he maintains a lifelong passion for prayers and poetry, particularly religious poetry. He is married to Yvonne and resides in Delray Beach, Florida.

Rev. Dr. Yvonne Martinez Thorne has an MDiv from Palmer Theological Seminary and an EdD in counseling psychology from Columbia University. She is an ordained clergy member for the American Baptist Churches USA and the founder and CEO of Cultivating Wholeness Counseling Associates, located in Pennsylvania and Florida. She is married to Leo and resides in Delray Beach, Florida.

Abbreviations

401(k)	Retirement savings plan that provides tax advantages to savers
AA	Alcoholics Anonymous
ABC	American Broadcasting Company
AD	Anno Domini
AIDS	Acquired immunodeficiency syndrome
Al-Anon	Derivative of Alcoholics Anonymous
a.m.	Ante meridiem (before noon)
CEB	Common English Bible
GMA	*Good Morning America* television show
KJV	King James Version Bible
MBA	Master of business administration
NIV	New International Version Bible
NRSV	New Revised Standard Version Bible
NRSVue	New Revised Standard Version Updated Edition Bible
p.m.	Post meridiem (after midday)

1

Gratitude Begins with God
Doug Hood

> *Though the fig tree doesn't bloom, and there's no produce on the vine; though the olive crop withers, and the fields don't provide food; though the sheep is cut off from the pen, and there is no cattle in the stalls; I will rejoice in the Lord. I will rejoice in the God of my deliverance.* —Habakkuk 3:17–18

In our nation's ritual observance of Thanksgiving Day, we are summoned to express gratitude for what we have. We may have little when measured against our neighbor, but we are, nonetheless, called to acknowledge what we do have and express gratitude. We know the story, the origin of this national holiday well. English immigrants—later to be called Pilgrims—sailed by accident into Cape Cod harbor, staked their claim upon the land, and named it New Plymouth. These immigrants, these Pilgrims, labored hard working the land, fought disease, and defended themselves against every threat this strange new frontier presented. Life produced struggle upon struggle. But they persisted. Then, in 1621, the harvest exceeded every expectation. To celebrate their good fortune, a harvest festival was held, to which they invited the native Americans who had occupied the land first.

A Month of Prayer and Gratitude

As a child, I would be reminded by my mother and father that Thanksgiving Day was an occasion to "count my blessings." As I consider this instruction, it seems to me that there is nothing wrong with a regular habit of doing so—counting my blessings. I have provided the same guidance to my children. Focusing on what I have versus what I don't have is a mindset that must be intentional. For some reason, I find that many of us have a default setting to do just the opposite. Many days, I am caught up in complaints—usually in silence. I don't have enough, whatever "enough" may be. If I dwell there long enough, I grow convinced that I have been cheated. If you have traveled this same route, you know it is an unpleasant journey. Then, I am reminded of the wisdom taught me so many years ago—count my blessings, regardless of how meager those blessings may seem to be.

The difficulty with this Scripture from the minor prophet Habakkuk is that it seems to invite us in the opposite direction. At first blush, this seems to be a well-rehearsed complaint: the fig tree doesn't bloom, and there's no produce on the vine, and on and on. Sounds familiar, like a child who is struggling through a difficult day. The only difference between the child and the adult is that many adults have learned restraint. We feel as strongly as the child about what we don't have, but we have learned to keep our lips sealed. Our lips may conceal what is on our hearts, but rarely is it a secret to others. When our lips are sealed, our general countenance betrays us. Others see our dissatisfaction, our annoyance, our general selfishness. Then, as we are reading the Bible, we stumble upon these words from Habakkuk. Permission granted for making our complaint! Or so it seems until we keep reading.

We are jolted by a speed bump in verse 18. After a considerable complaint, the prophet Habakkuk concludes with gratitude! A bleak and depressing picture is painted for us and is then completed with "I will rejoice in the Lord. I will rejoice in the God of my deliverance." It appears that someone has confused the lyrics of one song, a song of complaint, with the lyrics of another song, a song of gratitude. One doesn't follow another, not smoothly anyway. Failure and loss move rather quickly to a celebration of hope and confidence. How does the prophet explain this disjointed movement? It may be that we have gratitude all wrong. Perhaps gratitude doesn't begin with what we have. Perhaps gratitude doesn't even begin with us. If we lean into the pages of this prophet, what we learn is that gratitude begins with God, with God's fidelity, and that we are included in God's redemption. Gratitude begins when we realize we belong to God.

Precious God, giver of every good and perfect gift, I pause and count my blessings today: one, two, three, seven, fifty, sixty . . . And I smile in thankfulness! In your divine wisdom, you have given me what I need, not what I want. For this loving wisdom, I thank you. Righteous God, I never lack; my cup is more than half full. My grateful heart sings a melody of praise today that Jesus loves me. God of redemption and transformation, this is my greatest blessing of all—I belong to God! Praise be to God! In Jesus' name, I pray. Amen.

2

Meet Me at Ten Minutes to Seven in Your Heart

THOMAS K. TEWELL

> *When you pray, don't pour out a flood of empty words, as the Gentiles do. They think that by saying many words they'll be heard.* —Matthew 6:7

Have you ever promised someone, "I'll pray for you"... and then forgotten to do it? I have! Sometimes, I say that I'm going to pray for someone... but amid the busyness of life and ministry... I forget! Then a day later... I think of that person for whom I was going to pray... and my face turns red! So... I decided to adopt three habits that help me keep my promise. Maybe you will consider trying these habits, too!

Habit 1: Get specific. When I ask someone if they would allow me to pray with and for them, I ask them specifically what they'd like me to pray for. The specificity of their request has helped me enormously. Instead of offering a "general prayer" for someone, my prayer is in tune with the desires of their heart. And, when they give me something specific to pray for, I feel commissioned by them to pray . . . and I remember to do it! I also write their request down . . . that helps too!

Habit 2: A prayer bundle. One of my spiritual practices is to keep a daily prayer bundle of people for whom I pray. Here is how it works. I pray for some people every day . . . my wife, two sons, two daughters-in-law, and our grandchildren, as well as the members of our Macedonian Ministry staff team and other friends. They are in my daily prayer bundle no matter what. And, I sometimes ask one or more of them specifically, "Where do you need prayer right now?" They always seem to appreciate my asking. In addition, if I am working with a pastor on their preaching, leading a retreat for a church, or meeting with a cohort of Macedonian Ministry pastors, I put them in my prayer bundle. And . . . I take people in and out of my bundle as circumstances change.

Habit 3: Checking in. I check in with the person for whom I am praying, and I ask them about the specific things for which they asked me to pray. That way, I not only update my prayer bundle, but it reminds me to pray for them. I may send the person a text, an email, or give them a quick phone call to check-in. Checking in means a lot to people . . . and to me!

When I mentioned my "prayer bundle" concept at a retreat recently, two men introduced themselves to me whose lives have been radically changed by prayer. Bob and Jim had been roommates in college. After spending several years in the business world without keeping in touch, they met again in an MBA program. After getting their business degrees, they moved to Washington DC, married, started families, and had significant careers in our nation's capital. Although their lives were quite similar, there were several major differences . . . Bob was a person of faith who had admitted the fact that he was an alcoholic and was getting help . . . while Jim was not a person of faith, and to be honest, he had not yet faced his drinking problem.

In a time of crisis, Jim reached out to Bob for help . . . knowing that Bob was a member of Alcoholics Anonymous. As Bob shared with Jim the brokenness of his life and how he painfully came to the realization that he was powerless over alcohol . . . Jim realized that he had called the right friend. Jim shared his pain with Bob . . . pain that he had not shared with anyone. For the first time in his life, Jim said these words . . . and meant them . . . "I am an alcoholic." That very night, Bob took Jim to his first AA meeting. As they talked after the meeting, Jim said to Bob, "Now comes the hard part. I have to go home and tell my wife." Jim had actually tried telling her a few years earlier, but the words wouldn't come.

Bob asked, "When are you going to tell her?" Jim said, "I think I'll tell her after we take the kids to school tomorrow morning." Bob said, "Jim, is there any time that you will be alone between now and then?" Jim said, "The only time that I will be alone between now and telling her is when I get into the shower in the morning." Bob said, "What time is that?" Jim said, "I can set my watch by it. I get into the shower at ten minutes to seven every morning." Bob said, "OK, when you get into the shower, and the water pours down on your face, imagine that the water is the healing power of God. I know you have doubts about the God thing . . . I understand that . . . but trust me, whoever God is will be there to give you the words to say to Ann. And, remember . . . I will be praying for you at exactly ten minutes to seven."

The next morning at ten minutes to seven, the water came down on Jim . . . and nothing special happened. No lightning bolts . . . no voice from God. However, Jim did feel an inner assurance that he was doing the right thing by being honest with his wife. When he stammered out the words that he was an alcoholic . . . Ann got up from the table, came right over to Jim, and hugged him. She said, "Honey . . . I've known this for a long time, but I didn't know whether you knew it." Ann had been secretly going to Al-Anon meetings for spouses of alcoholics, but now Jim and Ann could face this challenge together. For the first time in his life, Jim thought . . . "There may be a God."

At the retreat, Jim told me that he believes in God . . . and he has been free of alcohol for over two years. He is starting to feel much better, but he knows that he has to say no to alcohol . . . one day at a time! Jim also told me that the key moment for him was when Bob told him that he was going to pray for him at ten minutes to seven! These men have been praying for each other at ten minutes to seven each morning for the past two years. They pray and check in about everything . . . their lives, their marriages . . . their roles as fathers . . . their careers. Everything.

The truth is that they are in each other's prayer bundles! They did not know what to call their practice . . . and I gave them a name for it . . . prayer bundles! That's why when I mentioned this at the retreat, they were eager to tell me their story. And, they wanted to tell me why it is so meaningful to them to meet every morning . . . at ten minutes to seven . . . in their hearts! Tell me . . . do you have a prayer bundle? And, do you have someone with whom you could pray at ten minutes to seven?

Dear God of mysterious and unsearchable ways, nothing is ever hidden from you, not even "that thing" I am hiding from myself. You are a loving God of miracles, and you want to free me from the burden I carry. Loving Savior, sometimes you prepare people, angels unawares, who are waiting to walk alongside us in compassionate concern. Open my eyes today to discern and welcome with gratitude any of your earthly messengers sent to help me hold it together. I am ready, Lord. I humbly pray in the powerful name of Jesus, my Christ. Amen.

3

An Attitude of Gratitude

MICHAEL B. BROWN

> *A joyful heart helps healing, but a broken spirit dries up the bones.*—Proverbs 17:22

I once heard the late Dr. Charlie White tell a humorous story about an elderly woman deep in the Ozark Mountains. She possessed very little in material ways but always maintained a spirit of thankfulness for what she did have. When asked to offer grace at a family holiday dinner (with a huge spread on the table), she bowed her head and said: "Dear Lord, as I look at this food, I find myself thinking, I may have only two teeth, but thank God they both meet!"

Laughter is good medicine, the Bible tells us (Proverbs 17:22). It can also be the source of deep wisdom, as in the story of that woman who said grace. An attitude of gratitude focuses not so much on the amount of possessions as on their quality. My dad was a man with that sort of perspective about things. As a teen, whenever I would return from a friend's house and remark to Dad about how big and beautiful it was, he had a standard answer: "You can't live in but one room at a time." Or, when I would brag (hint, perhaps?) about some buddy's new car and how great it was, he would say: "The purpose of a car is to get you safely from point A to point B. Yours does that, so it's a 'good' car." The older I grow, the more I understand the astuteness of his words.

This doesn't mean, of course, that we should denigrate nice things or fail to appreciate such things when we possess them. It is rather to say that anything that is useful, anything that brings joy or comfort, is a "nice thing." Think of Mary as Luke tells her story in the first chapter of his Gospel:

- She is an unwed young girl (probably in her early teens).
- She is betrothed (engaged in a legally binding way).
- She and her fiancé are not people of means.
- She is startled (Luke says "greatly troubled") by an unexpected angel who brings an equally unexpected message. Mary "will conceive and bear a son," though in her own words, she has "been with no man."

At that moment, Mary was sure of a handful of things:

- Joseph would neither believe nor understand this strange tale, and he would, in all likelihood, end their relationship.
- Neither his family nor her own would take her at her word.
- In her small town where everyone knew everyone else, her reputation would be ruined (she would be forever branded with a scarlet letter).
- Even her life could be in danger, as infidelity, when betrothed, was a capital offense should the betrayed party choose to pursue it.

No wonder that young girl was "greatly troubled." And yet, when she assessed the situation in its full context, when she focused on the angel's words, "Therefore, the one who is to be born will be holy. He will be called God's Son" (Luke 35:1b), Mary exclaimed not with fear but with joy: "Because the mighty one has done great things for me!" (Luke 1:49a).

Mary had every reason to envy others who possessed more or to lament the challenges that had been placed before her. But instead, she focused on the blessings, hope in the midst of hard times, and goodness located in a world of challenge. She realized it is not the quantity of one's possessions that matters, but rather the quality. And what could bring greater quality than to know she had a personal relation with "the holy one [who] will be called God's Son"? Her awareness of quality and her gratitude for it brought her a sense of deep joy. "The mighty one has done great things for me!" That's the place we always wind up if we cultivate attitudes of gratitude.

Faithful and loving God, help me to be gratitude ready today. I will choose to interpret all my steps and stops, my bumps and bruises, my abundance and scarcity, my joys and happiness through the lens of a heart grateful for all your blessings. You are my fortress, my life-giver, my faithful guide. Open my eyes to look around and be encouraged by saints like me who are seeking to be your Christlike lights in this broken and distracted world. Help me to learn the deep and hard lesson that my life with you sometimes comes with major disruptions. I will not always see clearly nor understand your loving and mysterious ways. I will humbly show up today. Here I am, Lord, in your presence, grateful for all your blessings and ready to see new opportunities for my life. In the powerful name of Jesus the Christ. Amen.

4

Foundations

Doug Hood

> *The Lord your redeemer who formed you in the womb says: I am the Lord, the maker of all, who alone stretched out the heavens, who spread out the earth by myself.* —Isaiah 44:24

Foundations are important. In the construction of a building, a strong and reliable foundation is a primary consideration. The function of the building and its location are important matters for determining which materials are necessary. Without attending to the matter of a proper foundation, further construction becomes a foolish—and risky—enterprise. Similarly, a meaningful and purposeful life requires a sturdy foundation. The materials for such a foundation include unconditional love, encouragement, and support. But other matters are important too! These include education or vocational training, a safe environment for failure and learning from that failure, and career guidance or mentoring. Yet, the most important matter is to know where we come from. Who are our parents? Were we adopted? What can we know of our heritage? Self-concept and identity are forged from this knowledge.

This passage from Isaiah shows that the people of Israel have lost their way. Their home, Jerusalem, has been destroyed, and they are a people in exile. Such disorientation is a poor foundation for rebuilding their future as a nation. It is in this disorientation, this emotional and spiritual place of despair and hopelessness, that the prophet Isaiah speaks. He reminds the people that they were formed in the womb by God—the same God who is the maker of all, who alone stretched out the heavens and spread out the earth. Israel, Isaiah cries, has not been left alone! And as a people who were created, fashioned, and formed by such a God, they are a people who *belong*. Isaiah reaffirms once again their relationship—their foundation—with their God. And it's this relationship that has continued on throughout the ages unto this very day.

Understand, however, that we shouldn't make the mistake of assuming that God belongs to *us*. Allan Hugh Cole Jr. shares a poignant metaphor he once learned that "acting as if God somehow belongs to us can have a direct effect on prayer and faith. For example, it can lead to our viewing God as a commodity that exists primarily to serve us and our self-interests, rather than leading us to serve God and God's interest. Moreover, we can begin treating God as 'a cosmic Coke machine,' such that we merely need to offer God some sort of payment (i.e., good deeds, the right prayers, acts of kindness, various sacrifices), put in our requests, and expect to receive something in return from God immediately."[1] This incorrect notion that our relationship with God is purely transactional is a poor foundation for a faith that can navigate life's discouragements and heartbreaks—it's a foundation that cannot sustain us.

A life of faith and prayer that disappoints may be the product of a poorly laid foundation. Instead of seeking a relationship with God, we might pray, "God, I will give you this if you give me that." Another poor foundation may be casting God in our own image rather than the other way around: we might depict God as an extension of ourselves, our desires, our needs, and our political ideology. We want God to see the world as *we* see it—we want God to be a certain way. This is a foundation that negatively impacts our prayers and shakes our faith. God does not operate under our control. As the prophet Isaiah reminds us, we belong

---

1. Cole, *Life of Prayer*, 15.

to God. The only foundation for a robust life of prayer and faith is one where we seek to know God, God's dreams, and God's aspirations—it is one where we remember that God has created us and not the other way around.

Living God, may the prophet's words that assure me of who you are and of who you are to me, my redeemer and friend, remind me today that you are my only true security and source of my deepest joy in this life, and that you have a blessed purpose for my life. You seek an abiding relationship with me, an imperfect human person, formed in your image and likeness. Continue to grow me in the belief that a vital and intentional life of prayer is indispensable for this relationship. Loving Savior, deeply I inhale this life-giving power that you are my center, my circumference, my foundation. I exhale in the gift of your glorious peace and in the life-giving joy of your unconditional love. This is the faith by which I live today in the redeeming power of Jesus the Christ. Amen.

5

Praying Like a Child

Nathanael Hood

> *At that time the disciples came to Jesus and asked, "Who is the greatest in the kingdom of heaven?" Then he called a little child over to sit among the disciples, and said, "I assure you that if you don't turn your lives around and become like this little child, you will definitely not enter the kingdom of heaven. Those who humble themselves like this little child will be the greatest in the kingdom of heaven. Whoever welcomes one such child in my name welcomes me."*—Matthew 18:1–5

Once in a priory in Paris, there lived a monk. A clumsy but well-meaning fellow, he'd left behind the secular world in his twenties to join the Carmelites, a Catholic order devoted to poverty and prayer. His life before the order had been a difficult one—born an impoverished peasant, he'd fought as a soldier in the cataclysmic Thirty Years's War, which decimated central Europe in the early seventeenth century. He saw much fighting, was once almost hanged by enemy troops, and was left lame by his injuries. Unable to remain a soldier, he began his new life of prayer and contemplation in 1640, taking the religious name "Lawrence of the Resurrection." Brother Lawrence's first ten years as a monk were difficult ones, which saw him battling feelings of guilt and unworthiness. But as the years crept by, he eventually surrendered himself to God's mercy and became a model monk. He spent most of his life quietly toiling away in the priory's kitchen, a job he initially disliked, switching to a less strenuous one only after one of his lame legs became ulcerated.[1]

Brother Lawrence died at the age of eighty in 1691 after a lifetime of service, but unlike most monks and nuns who live and die in historical anonymity, we remember his name and deeds over three centuries later. A collection of his letters and sayings were gathered together after his death by a cleric named Abbé Joseph de Beaufort and published as *The Practice of the Presence of God*, a remarkable little book that's been published in countless editions in several languages. The book is suffused with the insight and wisdom of a man whose "principle endeavor [was] to stay as close as possible to God, doing, saying, and thinking nothing that might displease him."[2] Indeed, it could be said he was a man who loved, worshiped, and prayed as a child.

But what does this mean, to love, pray, and worship as a child? For an answer, we turn to the eighteenth chapter of the Gospel of Matthew where Jesus' disciples come to Jesus with a question: Who among them would be the greatest in the kingdom of heaven? Jesus' answer took everyone by surprise, explaining that the greatest among them would be those who were most like a child. Part of the shock of Jesus' answer came from the lowly status children had in ancient Israel, but much of it came from the idea that adults should mimic children! Shouldn't it be the other way around? Children are loud, emotional, demanding, and often smelly! How could children possibly be a model of faith and piety? For that, I would answer that anyone who has spent a good amount of time among children knows that they don't do things by half measures. They love mightily, hate bitterly, feel deeply. To be like a child is to surrender oneself entirely and wholeheartedly.

---

1. Miller, "Introduction."
2. Lawrence, *Practice of the Presence*, 28.

A Month of Prayer and Gratitude

The great preacher and writer Harry Emerson Fosdick once wrote that "to pray to God as though he were Santa Claus is *childish*; but a man may still be *childlike* in his faith and range up into another sort of praying."[3] Put simply, to pray selflessly is childlike; to pray selfishly is childish. God wants us to offer up our earnest needs and desires in prayer, yes, but it should be accompanied by our total surrender to the Almighty. Just as a child rushes into a parent's arms, so must we rush into our Heavenly Father's arms when we pray. Consider Brother Lawrence. He could have done nothing but pray for healing in his legs or a better job outside the hustle and bustle of the kitchen—but that would have been praying selfishly. Instead, he prayed to know God in his every waking moment, both at rest and at work, in his strength and in his weakness. May it be so for all of us every day.

Gentle Savior, give me grace to frame my life in humility and in the spontaneity of childlike faith. This faith needs my constant care and my vigilance to surrender to your leading. Give me the freedom to walk with you in my joys and pains, in my steps and stops, in my weaknesses and strengthen, in my failures and successes. Merciful God, as you and I skip through this day, step by step, grant me the courage and freedom to expand my faith in the life-fulfilling joy of serving others. In the name of Jesus, the lover of children, I pray.

---

3. Fosdick, *Meaning of Prayer*, 22; emphasis in original.

6

Sarah's Purse

SUSAN SPARKS

> *And serve each other according to the gift each person has received, as good managers of God's diverse gifts.* —1 Peter 4:10

As a minister, you love everyone in your congregation. However, if you're honest, you have to admit that there are certain people you are especially happy to see. For me, that was Sarah Goodson. Raised during the Depression on a sharecropper's farm in the South Carolina low country, Sarah loved two things in this life more than anything: her family and taking care of people. She moved to New York City in the 1940s to give her family a better life and became a nurse to care for others. She made those two things a priority in every part of her life—down to what she carried in her purse.

I always loved to see Sarah coming into church with her big ole pocketbook because I knew what was in it. After each service during coffee hour, she would open her overstuffed bag and pull out the newest photos of her grandkids (not individual photos, but the old-school kind where you flip open the book and the photos unfold in zigzag plastic holders all the way to the floor). Then, as the picture albums were being passed around, little ziplock bags and Tupperware containers would magically emerge from that purse—bags full of fried chicken, collard greens, shrimp and okra gumbo, oxtail stew, hot corn muffins with blueberries, and, of course, peanut butter pie. One time I asked Sarah how she got all that stuff in her purse, and she told me about a gratitude ritual she performed every Saturday night. She would sit at her kitchen table, remove all the extra, heavy junk in her bag that she had collected during the week, then fill it back up with the important things for which she was grateful: photos of her grandkids and food to feed her church. It was a simple thing: cleaning out her purse. Yet it had such an impact, including the smiles on people's faces as they looked at the photos of the grandchildren and the comfort felt by all who ate that delicious food.

Perhaps we follow Sarah's lead and do a little Saturday-night purse cleaning of our own hearts. Let's start with this question: What emotional baggage are you carrying today that you should unload? Everyone's answer is probably different. I'm going to pick one that I bet most of us carry: worry. Easy to do, fixes nothing. Rev. Joyce Myers once said, "Worry is like a rocking chair, worry is always in motion, but it never gets you anywhere."[1] Worry can take over our lives, crowd out all things that matter, and even make us sick. But we have an alternative. We can clean out the purse of our heart and hand our worries over to a greater power. Jesus said, "Come to me, all you who are struggling hard and carrying heavy loads, and I will give you rest" (Matthew 11:28). Bottom line: worry or believe. You can't do both. Which leads to my next question: What will you put in the place of worry? What is important to you? For what purpose are you here? I suggest that we follow Sarah's lead in this too. When I had the great honor of performing Sarah's funeral after she passed away, the message that people shared over and over was that she had brought them joy and made them feel loved. Is there any greater legacy?

This week, do a Saturday-night purse cleaning in your life. Identify the things that are weighing you down emotionally, physically, or spiritually, and clean them out. Then, refocus on the things

---

1. Meyer, "Cause and Cure," para. 2.

that matter. Spend time with your family. Share photographs that make people smile. Stuff a ziplock bag of yummy food in your purse or pocket and share it with others. Bring a little love and joy to this hungry world. And do it today. As Sarah would say, "Life is too hard and too short to carry things that just don't matter."

Blessed God, invade the secret corridors of my willing heart and refresh it with the beautiful siblings of gratitude, love, and joy. I seek your help in this moment to give me wisdom to choose simple acts of delight that will radiate outward to bless and inspire others in your name. Precious Lord Jesus, I am seeking a way to bring quiet and peace to my often-anxious-filled heart and to enrich my daily, sacred journey with you. God of abiding hope, reach deep into me today, even into those dark areas I refuse to claim, and empower me to serve you and others in the urgency of today with love and joy as your obedient, grateful child. Thank you, God, in the name of Christ. Amen.

7

A Thankful People
Doug Hood

> *The peace of Christ must control your hearts—a peace into which you were called in one body. And be thankful people.—* Colossians 3:15

There is an unsettling moment in the novel *Girl with a Pearl Earring* by Tracy Chevalier. Set in the Netherlands in the mid-1600s, a family that struggles to have enough grieves the loss of a young daughter, Agnes, from a plague that griped their residential quarter of Delft. With a despairing shake of the head, the mother laments, "God has punished us for taking for granted our good fortune. We must not forget that."[1] The loss of a young daughter is tragic, particularly when the loss is due to a plague that outruns us. Yet, the loss is made even more tragic when one is gripped with a flawed notion of the character of God. A lack of gratitude does not stir the wrath of God; it does not move God to punish. Continuing from one generation to the next is a failure to grasp what God is up to on the cross—God's movement toward our brokenness is one of grace, not vengeance.

---

1. Chevalier, *Girl with a Pearl Earring*, 76.

A theme of Paul's correspondence to the church in Colossae is gratitude—one captured three times in three verses! However, this theme is not generated as a warning to the church. Rather, the invitation to gratitude is promised as an opportunity to break and finally diminish a culture of ingratitude that permeates our lives. Ours is a culture that seeks to grasp more and more as though there exists a scarcity of resources. Hidden deep within our consciousness is a fear that failure to acquire good things now will result in our missing out. The result is a growing hunger to acquire more. Fear grows that we may not have enough, exhaustion in our striving diminishes appreciation—even joy—in what we presently have, and a competitive spirit shapes a heart that results in dissatisfaction. Finally, we are consumed by this endless striving, our hearts are emptied of peace, and we become ungrateful, even unhappy, people.

Paul's antidote is gratitude—generating intentional thankfulness for God's good creation, for the gift of our lives and the opportunity to love and be loved, and for the gift of redemption from brokenness and sin. Cultivation of gratitude for the ordinary as well as the extraordinary moments available each day will break the culture of ingratitude that tightly secures us in chains. A simple lunch shared with friends, the laughter of children at play, and taking notice once again of the beauty of the earth—the seashore, lush mountains, or flowery meadows—grows upon our consciousness, and we question how we failed to enjoy them before. Moreover, we realize a movement away from a lonely and competitive pursuit of new riches and a movement toward a strong sense of community cohesion that marks us as part of something so much more than our individual lives—members of the body of Christ.

David L. Bartlett shares that in Decatur, Georgia, there is a church that might have been named with Colossians in mind: the Thankful Baptist Church. "Colossians claims that, as with Thankful Baptist Church, when we dress up for each day's work, we dress ourselves in Christ, with thanksgiving. In a religious marketplace that pushes happy Christianity, Colossians speaks a word for thankful Christianity." Bartlett advances his observation here that thankfulness is harder to come by than happiness but is immeasurably better. Vibrant churches—as well as vibrant disciples—understand the need for gratitude to guard from self-absorption and, finally, despair. Jesus' own prayers sparkled with expressions of gratitude. Each prayer cultivated, strengthened, and reminded him that God is the very center of our life. Bartlett suggests this prayer, "You have given me so much, O God—I ask but for one thing more, a grateful heart."[2]

Generous God of abundance, you have given us life to enjoy all your daily blessings. With your melodious symphony of love, you fill every nook and cranny of this beautiful earth and our often-distracted lives with your music deep in our souls. This bountiful display of your faithfulness often escapes my heart, a heart so manipulated at times to keep the focus on myself, my wants, and the stuff of this life. Blessed God, give me a fresh supply of your grace today to fill my heart with anthems of gratitude. I say, yes to your goodness. Yes! I'm a-coming, Lord, in your gift of being alive today and in the power of the cross of Christ, in whose powerful name I make this prayer. Amen.

---

2. David Bartlett, in Bartlett and Taylor, *Feasting on the Word (Year C, vol. 1)*, 163.

8

Never Too Many Stamps
Bruce Main

> *You are the light of the world. A city on top of a hill can't be hidden.... In the same way, let your light shine before people, so they can see the good things you do and praise your Father who is in heaven.* —Matthew 5:14, 16

"They are polar opposites," shared my host. We had just finished discussing his intentions for the retreat I was about to lead. Now, he wanted to talk about his family. "One is loving, outward focused, a joy to be around. The other is so self-centered and drains the life of us whenever she's around." I glanced at the clock on the wall. It was creeping close to eleven p.m., and I was beginning to feel the effects of a long day of travel. "Another cup of coffee?" He poured without waiting for a response. I could tell this conversation was not ending anytime soon.

"Why do people age so differently?" posed my new friend. A professor at a small liberal arts college, he was sharing some of the challenges he and his wife were facing with aging parents. "My mother-in-law is a piece of work," he continued. "And she's robbing the joy and life out of my wife. Everything is a crisis. Everything is about her and about making her life better. I mean, the things she's complaining about are so petty. Fortunately, she lives three hours away from us. But she's talking about moving close. That would be a disaster."

"Tell me about your mother," I beckoned.

"Completely opposite," he began. "To give you an example, she has eleven grandchildren. Each grandchild has gone through college." He paused for a minute and took another swig of coffee. "This is remarkable," he chuckled. "While in college, she would write to each grandchild every week and enclose five dollars. That's a lot of notes. That's a lot of five-dollar bills. That's a lot of stamps. Every grandchild talks about their grandmother with such fondness," he concluded. "They call her all the time. They check in on her. They give her credit for helping them through tough times."

"You are the light of the world," says Jesus at the conclusion of his most famous sermon we know as the Beatitudes. To a Jewish listener, these words would have been unsettling. After all, the Torah was the light. Jerusalem was the light. God was the light. This truth was affirmed through the prophets and the Old Testament. But Jesus flips the script and reminds his listeners—*you* carry the light of God. And we all know that light gives life. Only with light can living things grow and flourish. Receive God's light. Reflect God's light through your acts of love, gratitude, and generosity. The world needs you.

Blessed God, help me to show up in my life today as someone other persons will enjoy being around. I seek your grace to be the day brightener, the cheerleader, the encourager, the tolerant one, the silent Santa Claus. But, precious Savior, can I sustain this high-intensity lifestyle today, every day? Maybe not. Give me the spiritual insight to show my generosity your way: to be the bearer of your light reflecting your love through me. In the sustaining power of Christ, my light. Amen.

9

Borrowing Time for Prayer

Doug Hood

> *Jesus was telling them a parable about their need to pray continuously and not to be discouraged.* —Luke 18:1

Near the beginning of my present ministry, I placed a brass plaque on the pulpit, positioned just above the Bible. It reads, "The pulpit must be the grave of all human words," by Edward Thurneysen. We don't come to worship for human advice. If we did, a church service would be no different than a TED Talk. I need to be reminded each week that people come not for an expression of my opinion; they come for the word of God. Here in this teaching from Luke's Gospel, Jesus is telling a parable about an opportunity to pray continuously. Jesus believed in prayer. Jesus prayed often. Jesus now wants us to know that prayer is nothing less than approaching the presence of an infinitely holy God. It is an invitation received from God. We must sense the gravity of that invitation and not be relaxed about prayer. Thought, preparation, and intentionality are a more responsible response to God's invitation to prayer.

A shared difficulty with this approach to prayer is sheer busyness. A man I admire in my present congregation once told me that Jesus' invitation for regular, daily prayer was a "tall ask." He owned a business with nearly nine hundred employees. Regular demands upon him rarely left time for reading the Bible, a helpful daily meditation, and prayer. I sympathized and tried to understand. Yet, I also hear that God's claim upon us—God's claim upon the life of my friend—isn't negotiable. Jesus asks that we pray continuously. That isn't advice from the pastor. It isn't the opinion of a human. It is all Jesus. A hit-or-miss casualness toward prayer is simply unacceptable. Close attention to Jesus' life discloses that Jesus remained busy healing, teaching, and proclaiming God's kingdom. It would be an interesting debate between my friend and Jesus, which one of them worked harder.

What my friend failed to grasp is that the time borrowed for reading Scripture, a brief meditation, and prayer will not be lost from his work. The poise, steadiness, and increased wisdom granted from time with God each morning will be recompensed to him many times over. That great leader of the early church, Martin Luther, understood this. "Luther habitually prayed for three hours each day."[1] There is simply no substitute for the value added to each day after being steadied and strengthened by God. Bruce Larson, a Presbyterian pastor of another generation, once spoke at a conference I attended on the value of prayer in his life. He said that if he missed a day of prayer, he noticed the difference. If he missed several days of prayer, his family noticed the difference. If he missed three days, his friends noticed the difference. If he missed for a week, his congregation noticed a difference.

Bryant Kirkland shared in a sermon before the faculty and students of Princeton Theological Seminary something he once found on the wall of an army chapel. It said, "Nothing happens here unless you want it to."[2] Naturally, the question for each of us is, what do we want to happen by prayer? What Jesus found in prayer was less a power to effect miracles and more a presence—God's presence—that brought in generous measures of strength in weakness, encouragement in discouragement, and inspiration to

1. Buttrick, *Prayer*, 265.
2. Kirkland, "God's Gifts," 268.

reach for greater heights. More, Jesus found someone who would never abandon him. Anne Frank wrote that she was prompted to keep a diary simply because "I don't have a friend."[3] Jesus doesn't want that to be our story. Rather, Jesus desires to introduce to us, through prayer, a God who not only desires to draw close to us but will create in us a transformative story. Confidently, Jesus asks, "Pray continuously and not be discouraged."

Precious and loving God, when I deny myself the joy of daily seeking the beauty and inner stillness of your divine presence, I am placing something, or someone else, in that sacred spot. Idolatry is not a desire of my spiritual life with you, but I sometimes choose to have idolatrous moments. Keep reminding me, holy God, that your loving grace gives me an invitation to make my life a daily offering to you. I covet a life of continuous prayer, shaped by the power of your living Word in me. Give me the needed strength to intentionally seek this healthy practice of being in your divine presence. I pray in the name of Jesus. Amen.

---

3. Frank, *Anne Frank*, 6.

10

Profit, Loss, and Gratitude

Nathanael Hood

> *For what shall it profit a man, if he shall gain the whole world, and lose his own soul?*—Mark 8:36 KJV

In 2018, Michael Norton, a professor at Harvard Business School, co-led a study where over two thousand people with a net worth of at least one million dollars were interviewed about their personal happiness. Two of the questions that produced the most revealing answers concerned his subjects' self-satisfaction with their personal wealth. First, Norton asked them to rate their happiness on a scale of one to ten. Second, he asked them how much more money they would need to get that happiness rating up to a ten. As Norton explained in an interview with *The Atlantic*: "All the way up the income-wealth spectrum, basically everyone says [they'd need] two or three times as much."[1] One would imagine that at a certain point when money stops being an issue, when private planes become as negligible an expense as a morning cup of coffee, enough would be, well, *enough*. But, as Norton discovered, human psychology doesn't always work sensibly—or rationally.

---

1. Pinsker, "Reason Many Ultrarich People," para. 8.

Hood—Profit, Loss, and Gratitude

The idea that wealth can't buy happiness isn't a particularly new or novel revelation. After all, one of the most famous and enduring stories of the last few centuries—Charles Dickens's *A Christmas Carol*—centers on a miser whose insatiable hunger for wealth left him so miserable, lonely, and despised that it took an act of God to save him from himself. Or consider J. Paul Getty, the infamous founder of the Getty Oil Company who was once listed in the 1960s as the richest man on earth. He was so single-minded in his pursuit of wealth and so paranoid in clinging to it that he once famously forced his kidnapped grandson to pay him back the ransom money he spent—with interest!

There are many ways that the stories of Scrooge and Getty could (and perhaps should) be read as cautionary tales, but one of the most glaring involves their common lack of gratitude. Was Scrooge thankful as a young man with a successful job and a beautiful fiancée? No, he traded both for loneliness, a gloomy apartment, and a bigger bank account. Was Getty thankful for his grandson's recovery from kidnappers? No, he saw it as yet another business transaction. There have been scientific studies proving that cultivating gratitude results in improved mental health and personal happiness, but perhaps equally important is the idea that gratitude protects us from losing our very humanity in the search for wealth and success. Put another way, gratitude keeps us from becoming a Scrooge or Getty.

Shortly after he predicted his death for the first time in the Gospel of Mark, Jesus Christ gave a brief sermon to his disciples about the importance of taking up one's cross and following him. It's only a few verses long, but it contains one of Jesus' most startling teachings, namely that anyone who seeks to save their lives by their own power will lose it. What use is gaining the whole world, Jesus asks, if you lose your soul in the process? And indeed, looking at the lives of Scrooge and Getty we see two men who leveraged their souls a long time ago. Imagine how much a little gratitude could have changed the lives of Scrooge and Getty. Let us give thanks that there is still plenty of time for the rest of us to make the change.

A Month of Prayer and Gratitude

Ever-present God, gratitude brings in tow your beautiful gift of contentment, which teaches the heart to be satisfied with having little or much. God, gratitude saves us from ourselves and brings to us greater spiritual and personal gain. Help me to restructure my life, to cultivate and lead with a spirit of gratitude. Give me eyes wide open to seek opportunities to help someone today with a kind word or action, even when my first impulse is to turn away and put aside the more noble path of Christlike generosity and humility. I make this prayer in dependence on your unfailing strength and in the name of my Lord, Jesus Christ. Amen.

11

Work in Progress

Greg Rapier

> *Jesus told this parable to certain people who had convinced themselves that they were righteous and who looked on everyone else with disgust:* "Two people went up to the temple to pray. One was a Pharisee and the other a tax collector. The Pharisee stood and prayed about himself with these words, 'God, I thank you that I'm not like everyone else—crooks, evildoers, adulterers—or even like this tax collector. I fast twice a week. I give a tenth of everything I receive.' But the tax collector stood at a distance. He wouldn't even lift his eyes to look toward heaven. Rather, he struck his chest and said, 'God, show mercy to me, a sinner.'"
> —Luke 18:9–13

The big danger in comparing ourselves to others is that we often, even when we don't mean to, compare our worst with others' best. We compare the inner machinations of our hearts, our deep and hidden struggles, against the public-facing version of our peers, the pristine and polished, Instagram-filtered, highly curated, tactfully presented as reality but not really reality–versions of people we see online. Or at church. Funny how those can feel the same. I imagine most of us, if we're honest with ourselves, make these comparisons and wince. We feel less than, broken, and incomplete.

My first time at the Metropolitan Museum of Art in New York, I was absolutely flooded with stimuli—artwork stacked high to the ceiling, people everywhere you look, large tour groups hastily ushered from one room to the next, over two million square feet jam-packed with some of the finest art in the world. In one of the rooms—I couldn't tell you which because the place was a decadent maze—my friend, a resident New Yorker and de facto tour guide, completely froze. He looked up at a long wall stretched even longer by all the artwork on display. Among the ornate, centuries-old, immaculate compositions, one painting stood apart, not because of its perfection, but because of its flaws.

Much of the canvas featured precise, lifelike depictions of saints and angels and Jesus Christ, but in the upper left-hand quadrant, prominently positioned against a blue backdrop, rested two beige mannequin-like figures, sketched out but never completed. Part of the painting was missing. My friend leaned over and whispered, "I like this one because it's unfinished."

Jesus' parable in Luke 18 reminds us that we are all unfinished and that there's no sense in pretending anything else—not for other people, and certainly not for God. There's power in humility and dignity in vulnerability. This is how we ought to come before God and pray, not as perfect people but as works in progress, some quadrants of life more sketched out than others. Because when we do that—when we show up to pray not as our perfect selves but as our whole selves—we discover a God of infinite grace, a God who sees our flaws and loves us anyway, who says this messy, unfinished canvas of a life holds innate beauty and deserves to be displayed. The Scripture reminds us that we're all God's people, and that in God's great gallery, Jesus Christ has reserved a place for us all.

Merciful God, I need your help to never grow tired of wrestling with my imperfection. As Creator of all, you flawlessly formed

Rapier—Work in Progress

from earth's new dust this beautiful human person a little lower than the angels, but made in the perfect image and likeness of God. All-wise God of loving mystery, I confess that I remain bewildered during the best and worst versions of myself to grasp "this image thing"; I am humbled and dazzled even by the thought. You are not done with me yet, Lord, and I am not pleased with the inelegant way I sometimes choose to see my also-unfinished neighbor. With a heart filled with gratitude, I thank you that your eyes of grace see the potential and the realization of your perfection in me by the sacrifice of your Son—and in my neighbor as well. I make this my not-occasional prayer in the name of Christ. Amen.

12

The Christian Way of Life
Doug Hood

> *Rejoice always. Pray continually. Give thanks in every situation because this is God's will for you in Christ Jesus.*
> —1 Thessalonians 5:16–18

CliffsNotes is a series of study guides in pamphlet form. Great works of literature and other works are redacted—or condensed—to present a larger work in a more accessible form for a quick perusal of the material. Some use CliffsNotes to determine if a large work is something in which they want to invest the time in savoring the entire volume. Others, usually students preparing for an exam, simply want the facts. In these three brief verses from Paul's letter to the Thessalonians, Paul provides the CliffsNotes to the Christian way of life. In three rapid movements, God's will for us is presented: we are to be a people who rejoice always, who pray continually, and who give thanks in every situation. Paul met with this young congregation only a few times before writing this letter, yet he has developed a deep affection for them—"like a nursing mother caring for her own children" (1 Thessalonians 2:7b)—and longs that they grow strong in these three common shared experiences.

What does it mean to "rejoice always"? When my son, Nathanael, turned five years old, his mother and I threw him a birthday party. Half a dozen of his friends were invited, and as traditional birthdays go, birthday presents were presented and opened before cutting the birthday cake. Opening one gift, Nathanael's eyes grew wide with joy, and, looking intently at the toy, exclaimed with delight, "It's what I have always wanted! What is it?" Knowing what the gift is or the function of the gift was not important. Something greater was going on. Nathanael was surrounded by people who loved him, who cared to show up for his birthday, and even now were celebrating him. There was a party going on, and Nathanael was at the center of it all! Paul's entire ministry is an announcement that God has shown up for us and is active in all things. Though there will be much in life we don't understand, God stands with us in all life's circumstances. That is an occasion for rejoicing always!

To pray continually is not every moment but constantly, repeatedly, as an acknowledgment that God is standing right with us. Richard Rohr tells us that St. Francis used to spend whole nights praying the same prayer: "Who are you, O God, and who am I?" Rohr asks that we notice that St. Francis is not stating anything, is not sure of anything, but is just asking open-ended questions.[1] This is the prayer that Paul speaks of when he instructs us to pray continually. The continual notice that God is God, whatever that may mean, and that we are not, is humbling. Such prayer—a constant awareness of a God of infinite mystery—diminishes any notion that we are large enough or strong enough to face life on our own. There is tremendous freedom in that! We are not alone in this journey we call life. Whatever may come in our future is not solely dependent upon us. The great object of prayer is to get home to God even when we fail to receive from God compliance with what we ask.

Paul concludes his summary of the Christian life asking that we give thanks in every situation. The careful eye will distinguish between "give thanks *in* every situation" and "give thanks *for* every

---

1. Rohr, *Yes, and . . .* , 102.

situation." Even the smallest child has experienced enough to realize that life throws some things at us that one cannot reasonably be thankful for. What Paul is asking us is that a life that has mastered rejoicing always and praying continually is a life that knows there is more to come—that any hardship, any loss, or any suffering fails to have the last word. God is present in each moment of our life and continually seeks our good. God has determined in the resurrection of Jesus Christ to have the last word for us. It is a word of life abundant with God for eternity. William James writes, "The greatest discovery of my generation is that people can alter their lives by altering their attitudes of mind."[2] Paul asks that we alter our lives simply by relinquishing control over our outcomes in life and approaching all situations with a grateful heart that God moves us forward—even through the darkest shadows. Here, writes Paul, is the sum of the Christian life.

God of compassion, love, power, mystery. Your amazing grace has set me free to freely choose you as my faithful guide and friend. You walk lockstep with me in every situation. I want to grow more deeply in the spiritual awareness that you are present with me. You seek to enshrine your wise and loving purpose into my life, even when life's hard and shadowy moments throw me off balance. Remind me, my God, that constant prayer, arising from a thankful heart, keeps me nimble to a higher standard of living, and gratitude transports me to a deeper understanding of your unconditional love. I submit to your wise guidance today. In the name of Christ, I pray. Amen.

---

2. Nightingale, *Successful Living*, 174.

13

What Group Are We?
Grace Cameron Hood

> *As God's household, you are built on the foundation of the apostles and prophets with Christ Jesus himself as the cornerstone.* —Ephesians 2:20

In my neighborhood, we have a lot of birds. We have a big group of white ibis that spend hours rooting and pecking for worms. The theory is that when there are ibis around, there will be no hurricanes. Do you know what a group of ibis is called? It is a colony. I found this interesting and funny so I started looking up other names of animal groups. A group of ants is also a colony. A group of roaches is called an intrusion. Dolphins are a pod; fish are a school. Some of my favorites include hippos, known as a thunder, and rhinos, a crash. Parrots are a pandemonium, while eagles are a convocation. Our friends, the owls in their wisdom, are a parliament. Giraffes are a tower. My absolute favorite is a group of flamingos is called a flamboyance.

Each name reflects something about the individual participants. Roaches are indeed an intrusion that everyone in Florida knows and pays to have removed. It doesn't matter if you call them roaches or palmetto bugs; nobody wants to find them in their house. The wild parrots in South Florida are also aptly called a pandemonium as they go from branch to branch, screeching wildly. So, what about a group of people who worship God and come together every week? They are called the church. Just as the name of each group is a descriptor of members, the word church should also describe us.

The word church means "house of the Lord." In this space, we come together regularly, worship God intensely, sing, and hear music that soars to the heavens. We are instructed in who God is and what God wants in our lives. We participate in the action of giving, praising, thanking, serving, and hearing. This happens all around the world. I have been to many types of churches. My first memory is of an open-air church where we all sat on logs under palm branches in the Congo. I have also attended beautiful churches in the Congo decorated with woven clothes, high tin roofs, and long, hard benches. Gold-plated cathedrals in Brazil contrast to the small woven churches in the Brazilian Indigenous reservations. A plain building that is a Quaker church in Pennsylvania stands near huge megachurches that meet in hotels and schools. Stained glass windows are one of my favorite additions, which appear in old country churches in muted shades of orange and brown and culminate in the breathtaking windows in the Sainte-Chapelle in Paris.

What ties all these structures together is the word *church*, house of God. What characterizes this word around the world is a sense of gratitude. Gratitude for a place to be the people of God. Gratitude for the family of God that comes together in worship and praise. Gratitude for being able to stand up and be counted as part of the group of people that stretches around the world. Gratitude is known and shown as members of the church bend over to help each other, to accept and celebrate our differences, to open wide the doors, and make room for more people who call themselves members of the "house of God" or the church.

Dear God, thank you for this beautiful community of joy-filled and imperfect people with whom we join in worship and praise to you. Proud and grateful we are to call you Lord, and to be identified as members of your worldwide household. Your sacrificial love is the grace-filled bond that binds us together as ready and generous keepers of our sisters and brothers. Loving God, give us undaunted courage day by day to support and serve all people among us, and to never neglect the needs of all your beautiful and needy children around the world. May we daily show our gratitude for your redemptive love by living redemptive lives. Our heartfelt desire is to serve all people everywhere as servants of Christ's love. In the joy of serving our Savior and Lord. Amen.

14

Jealousy, the Enemy of Gratitude

NATHANAEL HOOD

> *After David came back from killing the Philistine, and as the troops returned home, women from all of Israel's towns came out to meet King Saul with singing and dancing, with tambourines, rejoicing, and musical instruments. The women sang in celebration: "Saul has killed his thousands, but David has killed his tens of thousands!" Saul burned with anger. This song annoyed him. "They've credited David with tens of thousands," he said, "but only credit me with thousands. What's next for him—the kingdom itself?" So Saul kept a close eye on David from that point on.* —1 Samuel 18:6–9

For almost a decade now, I've kept a personal practice of reading through the entire Bible once per calendar year. I do this with the help of an online guide that divides the entire book into 365 bite-sized chunks, each taking ten to fifteen minutes to read. This practice has deepened my relationship with God in ways I can scarcely describe, but it's also had the odd side effect of permanently associating certain parts of the Bible in my mind with certain parts of the year. For example, for me, January is synonymous with stories of God's creation of the world, of Noah and the ark, of Abraham, Isaac, and Jacob, and of Joseph's bondage in Egypt. Likewise, the coming of summer in June and July means the Psalms; the arrival of cold weather in October, the Gospels; and the month of April—the time I am currently writing this meditation—the epic saga of the kings of Israel.

The stories of these kings and the rise and fall of their kingdoms are some of the most dynamic in the entire Bible, full of battles won and wars lost, of secret prophecies and even more secret magics, of doomed families and lost lineages. Put simply, I've come to associate the month of April with stories that would make the greatest fantasy authors, from J. R. R. Tolkien to George R. R. Martin, green with envy. The crown jewel of these April stories—for me, at least—involves King David, the most famous and revered of the biblical kings of Israel. David, shepherd son and Goliath-slayer, father of Solomon and author of psalms, has one of the richest, most extensive narratives of any single character in the entire Bible. And, perhaps unexpectedly for such a towering figure, he spends much of his youth powerless and fleeing for his life.

I'll not summarize the whole story here—these meditations do have a word-count limit—but suffice it to say that soon after entering the biblical narrative, David finds himself at odds with King Saul, the first king of Israel, the man whose throne he would one day usurp. The Bible portrays King Saul as a tragic figure, a once-righteous man whose flaws—many of which could be interpreted by modern readers as mental illnesses—lead to his downfall and death. At first, he loves David like a son, welcoming him into his court and enlisting him as a warrior in his armies. But David's divinely guided success on the battlefield quickly curdles Saul's affections. In the eighteenth chapter of 1 Samuel, the situation comes to a head when, fresh from a military success, Saul's subjects sing a song comparing his and David's exploits on the battlefield, lauding the latter over the former. As noted biblical scholar Walter Brueggemann points out, "The triumph belongs to both of them . . . there is enough joy for both to share fully."[1] But instead

---

1. Brueggemann, *First and Second Samuel*, 136.

of sharing in this joy, instead of feeling gratitude for the excellent service of his subject, Saul becomes consumed with jealousy. From that point on, Saul never trusts David again. From that point on, Saul's days as king are numbered.

There are two powerful lessons here for those with ears to listen. First, jealousy cannot coexist with gratitude. It poisons our minds and short-sights our outlooks. Saul could have accepted David's success with gratitude—his victories strengthened his kingdom and humbled his enemies! But his jealousy warped an ally into a foe, one he would eventually hound into exile and lose his throne pursuing. Second, true gratitude isn't selfish; it's self-*less*. Gratitude that comes from a loving heart rejoices in the successes of others and doesn't wallow in self-pity. Self-pity leads to jealousy, which, as my April readings prove year after year, leads to self-destruction.

Blessed God, help me to push myself off center stage. Open my heart to be more loving and thankful for the blessings you have so generously given to each of us, although not one of us deserves anything from you. Cultivate in me a grateful heart, which I will strive to keep open and pure in the awareness of my own incompleteness, my own desire to win points over others, my own tendency not to be selfless, my own blindness at times to see myself as you clearly see me. Lord, help me to listen in love to the story of a hurting person today. I submit my spirit of jealousy to you. Make me more like Jesus, I pray. Amen.

15

When It Is Hard to Pray

Doug Hood

> *Early in the morning, well before sunrise, Jesus rose and went to a deserted place where he could be alone in prayer.*
> —Mark 1:35

One evening a member of the church came to see me on the matter of prayer. I had just finished a teaching about prayer, and she questioned a claim I made about the early church Reformer Martin Luther. Luther was known to rise early on days when he had much to do and spend extra time in prayer. The young woman found this practice counterintuitive. "How," she asked, "is it possible to spend more time in prayer when the day before you already demands much?" I shared that this was not unique to Luther; many church leaders before Luther and many following him followed the same practice. Despite exceedingly busy lives, Luther and others realized that their own power to meet the challenges of the day was insufficient. Prayer infuses each life with uncommon strength, encouragement, and inspiration for facing every claim and every responsibility placed upon us.

The question of the young woman is a common one. Her question is not to be confused with doubts about prayer or technique. Those are important questions, of course. But her question was simply the struggle of time. How does a busy life find the time for regular, meaningful time with God in prayer? Some who have been Christians for years have a faith that remains in its infancy because they have failed to take this question seriously—the question of making time for prayer. They are the ones who admit that they pray only occasionally and then only when they feel particularly troubled about something. Their prayer is utterly listless, repeating a few familiar words they may have been taught as a child. What these people fail to understand is that God cannot provide strength, power, and encouragement when we don't make room for God in our lives.

When we find it hard to pray, Jesus speaks to us, here in Mark's Gospel, of two common obstacles: the obstacle of time and the obstacle of place. Though the difficulties with prayer may be numerous, none can be properly addressed without first identifying a sacred place and time to be alone with God. Often, people tell me that their busy lives give them no time for regular prayer, though they clearly have made time to check their phones for the score of their favorite team, read the headline news, or simply play a video game. Additionally, no one who cares deeply for someone neglects to spend time with them. Time is found for the things that matter. Jesus found time by rising early in the morning, well before sunrise. Even five minutes with a brief devotional followed by five minutes of prayer prepares us to receive the things God most wants to provide us.

Jesus then addresses the obstacle of place. Rising early in the morning, Jesus went to a deserted place where he could be alone. Though quick moments of prayer between demands of loved ones, children, or work colleagues are better than not praying at all, such moments will not nurture the quality of faith that comes with praying consistently in a more disciplined fashion. That discipline begins with identifying a place where there are no distractions, a place where the mind might experience quiet, and a place to simply be alone with God. There is wisdom in the teaching of the Psalms: "Be still, and know that I am God!" (Psalm

46:10 NRSVue) It is astonishing how real God becomes when we consistently consecrate a particular place that is for God alone as we pray. The disciples asked Jesus to teach them to pray. Jesus teaches that effective prayer begins with time and place.

Dear God, when I was a child, I spoke like a child and understood like a child; I even prayed like a child. Thank you for those formative years and for all the precious people who loved and encouraged me. As an adult, I have become a more responsible person, and I strive to accomplish much in my waking hours. I pray for the strength and wisdom, merciful God, to seek regular and intentional times of prayer, which offers me the delight of touching the heart of God. As a mature person, serious about building a stronger relationship with you, I commit myself today to keeping a journal as a needful aid to building a faithful life of prayer with you. In the power and strength of Christ, I pray. Amen.

16

Life's Undertow

Yvonne Martinez Thorne

> *But God definitely listened. He heard the sound of my prayer. Bless God! He didn't reject my prayer; he didn't withhold his faithful love from me.* —Psalm 66:19–20

It was the night before my husband and I were to fly back home. We had enjoyed our Christmas holidays on the island of Tobago. The sunny days, lush tropical landscapes, the majestic Caribbean Sea, lagoons, tropical birds, and fresh coconut water had done much to restore me from the hustle and bustle of work and ministry. For some unknown reason, I could not fall asleep. After tossing and turning, I quietly got up, went to our patio, and began to pray. I then opened up my Bible. Psalm 66 drew me. I became curious about how verses 11 and 12 might apply to my life: "You brought us into prison and laid burdens on our backs. You let people ride over our heads; we went through fire and water, but you brought us to a place of abundance" (NIV). I quietly wondered if something was about to happen. Little did I know that I would soon be encountering such a moment.

We took our final swim before heading back to our cabana. The Caribbean Sea was at its best for swimming through the waves and bodysurfing. My husband and I swam together as we waited for the perfect waves. As we were nearing our time to get out of the water, my husband made a gesture that I interpreted as: "This wave is a beauty. Let's bodysurf it." What I did not know was that this wave was not one to engage. I began to bodysurf the wave when suddenly and immediately, I became caught up in an undertow. What was I to do? Just as I wondered what to do, I heard the word "surrender." And I did. The undertow violently tossed me to and fro. I was thrust up into the air perpendicular to the ground by the force of the waves. At one point, another wave slammed my head into the sand. After what seemed like an eternity, the undertow let me go and I wobblingly raised myself up and slowly walked to the shore and into the arms of my husband.

As we walked back to the cabana, I remembered the verses I had read. With tears welling up in my eyes, I knew that God had prepared me for what had unexpectedly happened. I had cried out, and he had answered me. He had brought me through an undertow and showed me an abundance of his love. I am ever so grateful to him.

As I reflected on what happened that morning, I came away with the thought that God sometimes allows undertows in our lives that we may experience our deep need and dependence on God and on his infinite love for us.

Undertows are powerful ocean currents. They form when receding waters from waves that have previously broken onto the shore merge together with incoming waves. Sometimes in our lives, we can experience the pull of undertows created by situations that come over us like waves breaking against our souls. They overwhelm us. Sometimes, we are able to face them and resolve them. At other times, the waves of life seem to break continuously against us and create an undertow, a powerful current that renders us unable to break free. The divine instruction remains the same: Surrender. "You let people ride over our heads; we went through fire and water, but you brought us to a place of abundance" (Psalm 66:12 NIV). These moments invite us to a deeper experience of God's love and goodness. With a surrendered heart, we overflow with gratitude.

There is an epilogue to this story, the miraculous. As I was wobblingly walking out of the water toward the shore, I became aware that I had lost my swimming goggles. I use them to protect me from losing my contact lenses while swimming. "Oh no!" At that moment, I realized that I had also lost my left contact lens in the power of the undertow. Flying home would be challenging, I thought. As I was raising my right hand out of the moving waters towards my face, my contact lens was miraculously on the tip of my right index finger, in a concave position, ready to be popped into my left eye! How did this lens remain on my finger in the churning waters? Surrender . . . miracles . . . gratitude . . . God's love!

Awesome God of the miraculous, you show up in our lives with beauty, joy, and delightful moments that gently flow over our being. Your waves of blessing display your deep love for and delight in us. You are always "happening" in our lives. Open my eyes to see clearly that you are in every moment of our existence. Give me the peace and calm of surrender when life's billowing waves curl around me. Keep my anxious spirit open to experience with joy and thankfulness the mystery of your abiding presence in unexpected places. Inspire me daily to let my light shine so that others may see you and the beautiful wholeness available in your unconditional love and grace for all of us. In the beautiful name of Christ, I pray. Amen.

17

Summons to Gratitude

Doug Hood

Truly God is good to Israel, to those who are pure of heart.
—Psalm 73:1

The creation story of Genesis summons God's people to gratitude. The Lord took Adam, the first man of God's creation, and placed him in the garden of Eden to farm and take care of it. Additionally, Adam is invited to "eat your fill from all of the garden's trees" (Genesis 2:16b). Yet God's abundance did not end with an orchard. God realized that being well fed isn't enough. God declared it was not good for Adam to be alone. So, God fashioned a woman and brought the woman to Adam, who embraced her as his wife. Together, they would share in the goodness and abundance of God. For this, Adam and his wife were created. For this, Adam and his wife were summoned to gratitude, and in this gratitude, they would find their happiness. Gratitude is how we measure what is made available to us, however much or little it may be. It is a spirit that positively shapes us and folds us into a life of faith.

The Seventy-Third Psalm celebrates this summons with a ringing declaration, "Truly God is good to Israel, to those who are pure in heart." But as the psalmist continues to write, we discover that gratitude had nearly been lost for a moment. Immediately after the bold declaration of the first verse, there is a confession that the psalmist's feet had almost stumbled. The cause is quickly identified: Human eyes had turned away from what God was providing to look upon the prosperity of another. Comparison is measured between what we have and what another enjoys. The result of this comparison is a perceived imbalance—the other has more! Jealously poisons the heart, and bitterness, or anger, or both press against a heart once pure. This sight of another's prosperity created a sickness of heart and fueled a cynical spirit. And the psalmist's feet nearly stumbled beneath.

The antidote to this sickness, to this cynicism, is then announced: The psalmist went into the sanctuary of God. Eyes were directed away from another and their prosperity to see God once again. In prayer, in reading the Bible, and in worship, we are reminded once again that we deserve nothing. Yet, in God's grace, we have. We may have little or much, as the apostle Paul declares in one of his letters, but we have. Eyes directed back to God returns to us a true perspective—to view life, as it were, through the eyes of God. In the creation story of Genesis, Adam is placed in an orchard. Yet, careful attention to the story reveals that Adam is not to eat of one tree. Though this detail holds rich theological implications, let this one thing be understood: we were never created to have it all. Eyes turned away from God strive for much. But eyes turned toward God release gratitude for what we already have.

The Bible's summons to gratitude does not minimize the pain of loss and disappointment. Each is experienced during life, though some may experience both in greater measure than others. There are people who have longed to marry and never do. Others have wrestled with the loss of marriage, either through divorce or the death of a spouse. Health challenges or the loss of a child challenge the maintenance of a robust faith. The apostle Paul speaks of an unnamed "thorn in the flesh" and asks God on three occasions that God remove this pain from him. God does not. What is important is that Paul turns his attention from his struggle to focus on something beyond himself—the building of the church. Paul demonstrates that experiencing gratitude is possible only when one can direct attention from what one lacks to the presence of God. And God promised Paul that God's grace continued to abide.

O God of abundant grace, help me to shift my perspective today. My soul's desire is to live through the hours of this day turned toward you. May the spirit of a grateful heart, blessed God, help me to focus on what I have, and not on what others have. Help me to value my spiritual life of faith and my daily relationship with you as my most precious gift. Center my spirit on your abiding presence and grace in me. May this desirable field of vision purify my ever-so-willing heart, encourage a life of gratitude, and stir up in me a life that flows out in selfless service to others, who live adrift in a personal wilderness in your beautiful world. Lord Jesus, in your beautiful name, I pray. Amen.

18

Praying New York–Style

BRUCE MAIN

> *Stay alert and pray.*—Matthew 26:41a

I remember a story I once heard about one of Pastor Hood's mentors and role models—the Reverend Bryant M. Kirkland, who pastored the acclaimed Fifth Avenue Presbyterian Church in New York City from 1962 to 1987.

One September day, a Princeton Seminary student boarded the commuter train at Princeton Junction, New Jersey, to downtown Manhattan. This master of divinity student was to attend a lunch meeting with Reverend Kirkland at the New York Athletic Club to discuss his ministry field placement. Awed by the marble floors and stately columns of the eating establishment, the student nervously navigated his way past the receptionist to find Pastor Kirkland sitting at a white-clothed table adorned with silver utensils and glass goblets—a vivid contrast to the rather austere seminary cafeteria.

"Have you ever prayed New York–style?" stated Kirkland, as the lunch arrived.

Perplexed and bewildered, the student cast his eyes downward and sheepishly whispered, "No, sir."

Main—Praying New York–Style

"In New York, we pray with *our eyes wide open*," began Kirkland, scanning the large dining room fully attentively. "Dear Lord, we pray for the waitress serving us today, lift the burden she seems to be carrying. And for the businessmen at the back table, we pray the decisions they make will be just and fair for their employees. For the couple to our left who seem tense and at odds, we pray for their marriage." Then Kirkland paused and looked at the young seminarian in the eyes: "And God, thanks for my new friend. May our friendship be as delicious as the food we're about to receive. Bless him. Guide his steps as he studies to be the preacher and pastor you have called him to be."

Prayer is not simply closing our eyes and reciting our wish list to God. Prayer is opening our eyes to what God needs us to see now and responding with grace, empathy, and love. That's New York–style prayer—praying with our eyes wide open.

God of limitless and overflowing grace, teach us to pray, how to pray, and for whom to pray with eyes wide open to your Spirit, present and sometimes not-so-quietly moving all around us. Above all, ever-present God, impress upon me your loving inclusiveness and your compassionate love for this broken world into which you have called me to serve with unscripted, unorthodox, and holy awareness, all in Jesus' style. Amen.

19

Write Them on Your Doorframes
Nathanael Hood

> *These words that I am commanding you today must always be on your minds. . . . Tie them on your hand as a sign. They should be on your forehead as a symbol. Write them on your house's doorframes and on your city's gates.*—Deuteronomy 6:6, 8–9

Throughout the world, if you visit a religiously observant Jewish household, you'll likely notice a tiny tilted cylinder called a mezuzah affixed to their doorposts. Usually no more than a few inches in size, a mezuzah—or the plural mezuzot—is commonly inscribed with nothing but the Hebrew letter ש, an abbreviation for the word *Shaddai*, which both Jews and Christians will recognize as one of God's many names in the Bible. With a handful of exceptions, mezuzot are placed in each doorway within a Jewish household. These mezuzot are not solid talismans but hollow containers holding a parchment scrape inscribed with verses from the Torah, the first five books of the Old Testament. There are many rules and regulations surrounding their construction, installation, and maintenance—only a *specific* kind of parchment can be used, the verses must be written by a *specifically* trained scribe, they must be affixed within a *specific* time frame after moving in, a *specific* blessing must be said as they're installed, and they must be *specifically* checked for deterioration or damage every few years.

For religious outsiders, this might seem quite the hassle! After all, when observant Christians put up crosses or crucifixes in our homes, we don't usually have a clergyperson make, install, and maintain them! But for observant Jews, mezuzot are not simple ornaments—they fulfill one of the 613 mitzvoth or "commandments" required of them in the Torah, specifically the command from the book of Deuteronomy to affix God's words to their "doorframes and on [their] city's gates." What respect! What piety! What *gratitude*. And "gratitude" is the proper word here, for the bestowal of the Torah and its 613 mitzvoth is considered by Jewish people as cause for joy and celebration. Mezuzot, therefore, are not grim, compulsory reminders of religious doctrine but everyday reminders of being God's precious covenant people.

As early Christianity diverged from traditional Judaism in the first and second centuries AD and became a religion dominated by gentile converts, we discarded most of the 613 mitzvoth—including the use of mezuzot. But there are times when I wonder whether Christianity may have lost something precious by abandoning them. I think, in particular, of a dear friend in New York City who identifies as Modern Orthodox and has mezuzot posted all throughout his apartment. I'm always deeply moved by how he'll reverently touch them as he passes them by, lifting his hand to his lips to kiss the fingers that themselves have touched God's words.

Understand this—I'm not advocating the Christian "reclamation" of mezuzot, but I do believe we stand to learn from our Jewish neighbor's model of everyday religious gratitude. Too often, we Christians limit our devotions to one hour of worship on Sunday morning and to prayers before meals and bedtime. But if the promises of the Gospels are true—if we *truly* are redeemed from sin through Christ and guaranteed everlasting life—why shouldn't we express a similar kind of gratitude? A joyous, sometimes euphoric everyday gratitude of amazement that, sinners though we be, we too have been chosen and redeemed, blessed and protected, cherished and beloved? So, while we maybe shouldn't affix Gospel verses to our doorposts, perhaps we Christians should strive in our own way to keep our gratitude alive and fresh all the days of our lives, in all our comings and goings. What other proper response could there be for a redemption such as that earned on the cross?

Most loving God of every detail of my life, help me to create by your Spirit, daily and visible rituals to express my gratitude for the loving transformation you brought into my life. I am transformed by your grace, and my life has become a living parchment, a spiritual testament, available to be read by all people. Help me to humbly express this holy letter in my soul in joyous and grateful ways. I sing an anthem of praise to you for your amazing gift. In the incomparable power of Christ, I stand. Amen!

20

God's Apparent Inattention to Prayer

Doug Hood

> *How long will you forget me, Lord? Forever? How long will you hide your face from me?*—Psalm 13:1

The critic Guy Davenport wrote that translation is a game of two languages, and that "the translator is in constant danger of inventing a third that lies between."[1] The language of the Christian faith is often characterized as one where God is responsive to prayer. The language of lived experience suggests that, on occasion, God is inattentive to prayer. What is the translator to do—how does a person of faith translate a "responsive God" to the occasional experience of an "inattentive God"? Often, the translation—or explanation—is that the prayer lacked sufficient faith or that the prayer failed to follow some prescribed rubric or pattern. The tragic result is a third language, a God that is responsive only if the prayer has been constructed properly or is undergirded by an unwavering and sturdy faith. The third language is unrecognizable to the people of

---

1. Wood, "*Iliad* We've Lost," 83.

the Bible, particularly the psalmist. It is a language that suggests that effective prayer is dependent upon us, not God.

Psalm 13 is the shortest of the prayers that seek help from God in the book of Psalms. At the beginning of this prayer is a rhetorical question, "How long?" The question is asked four times in the first two verses. Information isn't sought. A response is sought from a God that seems unresponsive. The individual who makes this prayer is in distress. An urgent neediness is presented to God, and the expectation is that God will show up and answer, consistent with the understood character of God. Excuses for God's inattentiveness are not offered; God is not let off the hook. This is a powerful witness of refusal to inventing a third language. God is known as a responsive God. So, where are you, God? As James L. Mays makes clear, "God does not help; there is no evidence of God's attention and care. Anxiety tortures the mind with painful questions."[2] The named experience resonates with our own when we are impatient and desperate. Our questions about God's apparent inattention are not unfaithful.

It is important that the reader—the one who is eavesdropping on this urgent prayer—understand that the psalmist is not releasing their frustrations upon another. It isn't unusual for the faithful to speak to another of their disappointment with God. Many times, that is the preferred approach—sharing with a friend, rather than directly to God, a disappointment or hurt with a God that seems inattentive. This seems safer, less dangerous, than a direct and frank conversation with God on such matters. What is suspended in such moments is the recognition that nothing can be kept from God. God is privileged to our conversations as well as our thoughts. Just as Adam and Eve sought to hide from God, we participate in the self-deception that we can vent our frustrations about God to another without God's knowledge. Why risk stirring God's anger with such a blunt approach? Here, the psalmist does. God has let them down, or so the psalmist believes. Why not an honest conversation with God?

---

2. Mays, *Psalms*, 78.

This bold move, this courageous exercise of faith, in turning directly to a God who seems inattentive, grants permission to the reader to do the same. The psalmist's unflinching honesty before God demonstrates a confidence in God's love and care for the well-being of the faithful. This nervy move reminds the reader of another man of God named Job. Job never flinched before God in demanding an answer for his suffering. The answer never came to Job. Yet, in time, God does demonstrate faithfulness to Job with the return of good things. What we find in Job's story is that the individuals who feared holding God accountable received God's rebuke. The psalmist in this prayer doesn't receive an answer either. What to do with God's apparent inattentiveness? The psalmist chooses gratitude. "Yes, I will sing to the Lord because he has been good to me" (Psalm 13:6). Choosing to give up on God was not an option for this one who asks God, "How long?" Such a choice only results in a life of despair.

God of steadfast love, all knowing, all wise, my prayer awkwardly streams out of my lips today as honestly as I can utter them from my all-too-imperfect human heart. Sometimes I question if you are really paying attention to me in my moments of crisis. I seek your help, blessed God, with my stubborn need for certainty arising from within my anxious heart. With all the knowledge I possess, with all the skills I can draw from, with all the human contacts I know, I confess that I find no answer. Where are you, my sweet Lord? Be patient with me as I grow in the belief that I am not a victim of circumstances. I will not be overcome by this passing storm; you love me too much for that, and your faithfulness never fails. I pause and wait in the silence of a grateful, slightly open, but trusting heart. Amen.

21

Mark Twain's Favorite Word

THOMAS K. TEWELL

> *Rejoice always. Pray continually. Give thanks in every situation because this is God's will for you in Christ Jesus.*
> —1 Thessalonians 5:16–18

When Mark Twain was the most well-known and respected writer in the United States, he was paid five dollars for every word he wrote. Someone sent him a note that said, "Dear Mr. Twain, please send me your best word," and enclosed a five-dollar bill in the envelope. Mark Twain sent back a one-word response . . . "Thanks!"

Thanks really was Mark Twain's favorite word!

In the passage from 1 Thessalonians 5, the apostle Paul encourages us to give thanks in all circumstances. Notice that Paul didn't say, "Give thanks *for* all circumstances!" The reason we give thanks is that God is with us in all circumstances! We give thanks that the same God who raised Jesus from the dead, and who guided us in the past, will guide us in the future. We give thanks that we are not alone as we face challenging situations . . . God is with us! Even when we feel that God has abandoned us, and we think that God has forgotten about us . . . God is with us! It is important to open our eyes and focus on God and not on the circumstances! This is especially true when the circumstances seem overwhelming!

This was the case in the 1630s in Germany when the Thirty Years' War was raging throughout Europe. The walled city of Eilenberg, Germany, was so overrun with refugees, wounded soldiers, and unsanitary conditions that infection and pestilence broke out in waves and spread uncontrollably. In the year 1636, the plague hit! That was when a thirty-one-year-old minister and a native of Eilenberg, Rev. Martin Rinkart, was assigned by the Lutheran bishop to serve the Lutheran parish in his hometown. He was the only minister who survived the plague! So, he served the parish churches throughout the city as a solo ministry! Imagine the load that he carried in those years! And as one who had grown up there, Martin knew most of the citizens of Eilenberg who were dying. There were so many deaths in the city that Rev. Rinkart led as many as ten funerals and memorial services every few days!

During this bleak period, Rinkart did not focus on the tragedy of the circumstances . . . he got up every morning and he focused on God! He focused on what God was doing. How do I know? In 1636, Rinkart wrote one of the great hymns of our faith, "Now Thank We All Our God," that focused on Mark Twain's best word . . . thanks! Rinkart focused on the presence of God and the love and support of the congregations in those tumultuous times and not on the tragic deaths or the circumstances. The first two stanzas bear witness to a God who remained steadfast in a time of tragedy and unanswered questions.

> Now thank we all our God with heart and hands and voices
> Who wondrous things hath done, in whom this world rejoices;
> Who from our mothers' arms hath blessed us on our way
> With countless gifts of love, and still is ours today.
>
> O may this bounteous God through all our life be near us,
> With ever joyful hearts and blessed peace to cheer us;
> And keep us in God's grace, and guide us when perplexed,
> And free us from all ills in this world and the next![1]

1. Martin Rinkart, "Now Thank We All Our God," st. 1–2, in Presbyterian

Martin Rinkart was honest enough with his feelings to admit that he was perplexed about the circumstances, and he wondered out loud during his daily prayer and memorial services, "Where is God in the midst of this tragedy?" But as he wrestled with God and wondered about God's presence and God's seeming absence, Martin's focus was still on God's provision of comfort in this life, and eternal life in the next. This hymn is a powerful testimony to Mark Twain's best word . . . thanks!

I have a dear friend who is a Jewish rabbi. The rabbi urges his congregation to give thanks for one hundred things every day. And, with a twinkle in his eye, he tells them that if they can't think of one hundred things for which they are thankful, they should open their eyes. The rabbi is quite right. God is at work in all circumstances. But we don't see God at work because our focus is on the severity of the circumstances and not on God!

When we ask God to open our eyes and we start to see God at work, even in overwhelming circumstances, then we will have no problem giving thanks daily for one hundred things! And, when that happens . . . like Mark Twain, thanks will become our best word too! May it be so!

Almighty God, deep in my heart, I thank you for your unfailing faithfulness and goodness in all the varying circumstances of my life. I believe in your sustaining presence in all the vicissitudes of my earthly existence, though often perplexed I am. I believe in your transforming power. I believe in your voice of hope and assurance. Merciful Savior, today I feel overwhelmed and alone in my anxiety. God of hope, God of love, help me to remain steadfast in the sufficiency of your grace, to put on a smile to cheer up someone, to face this day with holy amazement, to see by faith beyond what my eyes can see, and to live above my humanity. I will live today in the power of Christ. Thank you, God. Thank you. Thanks. In the name of Christ, I make this prayer. Amen.

Church U.S.A., *Presbyterian Hymnal*, #555.

22

Thanksgiving in Bonaire
Doug Hood

> *After giving thanks, he broke it and said, "This is my body, which is for you; do this to remember me."*—1 Corinthians 11:24

This year, my wife, Grace, and I will celebrate Thanksgiving Day on the Caribbean Island of Bonaire. Our thirty-fourth Thanksgiving together, this one will be different. Most of our celebrations of this holiday have been with family—our children, our parents, or our siblings. Some years ago, our children and Grace's mother celebrated Thanksgiving with us in New York City, kicking the day off with the Macy's Thanksgiving Day Parade. During our twelve years in Bucks County, we shared a number of celebrations with another family in that church, each year alternating homes for the meal. Since moving to Florida, several celebrations were with a family of this congregation, breaking from meal preparation in the home to celebrate over a sumptuous buffet provided by the former Marriott of Delray Beach. Guests around the table may have varied through the years. However, there were always guests.

This year, neither of our children is able to make the trip to Florida. Our daughter, Rachael, has now made her home in Seattle,

A Month of Prayer and Gratitude

Washington, and our son, Nathanael, will be preparing final papers for the fall semester at Princeton Theological Seminary. My brother, Wayne, and his wife, Nancy, have now retired from their ministry in Florida and have moved to Tennessee, and Grace's siblings will be out of the country. The church family we shared several meals with at Marriott has moved on, and Grace and I have buried both of our parents. This year, Grace and I will be alone on Thanksgiving Day. It is a familiar story. Each year brings change to every one of us—and our families. Since the beginning of the pandemic, it seems the speed of change has only accelerated. Disorientation is the result, often accompanied by some level of grief.

This year's celebration will be a significant departure from our first thirty-three together—a holiday that always included either family or friends at the table. Therefore, Grace and I will celebrate Thanksgiving Day in Bonaire. It is a decision to embrace what is inevitable in all of our lives—change—and to make imaginative use of that change. Most of us have little control over our future. Change is a reliable companion that shares life with all of us. What we do have is the ability to take charge of that change and to make creative use of it in a manner that creates blessings. Without purposely choosing how we will adapt to change, the consequence that results may produce sadness and grief that are difficult to navigate. The inevitable change in the seasons of life may produce a deeper, richer experience than we ever thought possible, or it can diminish life. The choice belongs to every one of us.

Therefore, this year, Grace and I are going to Bonaire. Moreover, I have purchased a fruitcake. Not any fruitcake. Like many people, I usually do not care for fruitcakes. However, for decades I have delighted in the fruitcake from Collin Street Bakery in Corsicana, Texas. It has become a Thanksgiving Day tradition, and it is hard to imagine Thanksgiving without it. I will take this fruitcake to Bonaire and, only there, remove it from its packaging and enjoy it. This year, Thanksgiving Day will be a significant departure from previous celebrations. That is why this fruitcake is so important. In the midst of inevitable change, I need to remember—to remember the journey that now takes me to Bonaire. This fruitcake will connect me meaningfully to the richness of the past as I experience the present moment and anticipate the Thanksgivings that lie in the future. "After giving thanks, he broke it and said, 'This is my body, which is for you; do this to remember me.'"

Amazing God of holy contradictions, forever you are God, existing in unchanging permanence. Yet, you did change your eternal status and become like us, time-bound humans, to live among us mortals in changing, finite time. Divine disorientation, love's mysterious Magnificat! Above all, thank you for the gift of change, which can lead me to deeper experiences of renewal and a richer life with you, my God. Gracious God, keep my heart filled with thanksgiving for the mystery of your broken body alive in me today, and every day. I hold my arms outstretched in joyous praise. In the goodness of Jesus, my Lord, I pray. Amen.

23

More than Conquerors

YVONNE MARTINEZ THORNE

> *No, in all these things we are more than conquerors through him who loved us.* —Romans 8:37 NRSV

"Dr. Martinez, give me hope. We need hope." These heart-piercing words were uttered by one of my patients in a state psychiatric hospital where I worked as a budding psychologist. I had just finished a psychoeducational session with a group of patients when these words filled that room. As those words lingered in the silence and heaviness in the room, they began to stir something within me. What more was he asking for that I had not provided in the group session? Here was my patient, who usually remained silent, planning his next escape from the hospital, daring to speak these words to others and himself.

I had given him and others in the group what I had perceived as the needed information about substance abuse and mental illness. Yet, his question revealed that what I had presented did not address a deeper need coming from his searching and desperate heart: *a deep need for hope.* As I wrestled with his request and ensuing questions, I reflected on my own training to give hope and people's need for hope.

At the beginning of my brother's life-threatening illness, my family rallied around him, surrounding him with love and hope. Although we had never experienced terminal illness in our family, we were committed to walking alongside our dear brother, no matter the cost. We showered him with loving thoughts, inspiration, and emotional and physical support. As time passed and as the disease progressed in his body, we all found it difficult to sustain hope, his and ours. One day during a visit, he angrily cried out to me: "Don't put me in the ground. I am not dead yet!" His words registered in my heart that he was reaching out for hope. His words pierced my soul much like my patient's words did for me that day some months later.

My brother needed hope from his family to continue his journey in hope and in faith, even though we all knew that his life was coming to an end. Truth be told, in these two most challenging years, my family and I became more keenly aware of the power of God's amazing grace, God's unconditional love, and God's abiding presence with us even in end-of-life situations. We were taught valuable lessons about hope, which gave us all a deeper understanding of gratitude in situations that seem to be without hope and in moments of exquisite pain. Hope can light a path to gratitude, if only we choose to remain open and believe in God's wise purpose for our lives.

Let me put the matter this way. As my dear brother made his way into his eternal home, my family and I experienced the power of faith, compassion, and love that led to the emotional, relational, and spiritual healing we all needed. We learned that when we love as Christ taught us to love—deeply, selflessly, and sacrificially—we are able to reach into the bottomless depths of our capacity to love. This is a life-enriching gift. My family came to understand the apostle Paul's reminder to the Christ followers in Rome during their times of unrelenting persecution: "We are more than conquerors through him who loved us." (Romans 8:37 NSRV). My brother's sad end became an experience where we all saw our beloved brother fight for his good death in his home with his loved ones surrounding him. With Christ as our hope, we are more than conquerors as we live this life that, at times, asks of us more than we can bear. And, as we struggle in life, and as we grow in our ability to see God in these difficult times, we are able to discover the amazing and faithful love that God has for us, no matter what! For this, I am truly grateful.

The funny thing is, teachers have confessed that they often learn from their students; pastors acknowledge that they learn from their parishioners; psychologists, too, learn from their clients. Gratitude shows up in some strange and wonderful ways.

Eternal Life-Giver, your inscrutable ways are past finding out, but you never leave us in total darkness. The light of faith is the lamp that opens our eyes to see you, the blazing Light of our lives that does not consume, but enlightens us, even in our most painful and challenging human circumstances. Merciful God, daily increase our faith, hope, and love. And of these three, we pray most for the greatest of them, love—for you and for each other. Hope keeps us on the journey; gratitude provides joy-filled strength along the way. We celebrate and give abundant thanks for your life in us now and at the hour of our death. In the name of our resurrected Christ, we pray. Amen.

24

When You Don't Know How to Pray
Doug Hood

> *In the same way, the Spirit comes to help our weakness. We don't know what we should pray, but the Spirit himself pleads our case with unexpressed groans.* —Romans 8:26

Fyodor Dostoyevsky creates a vivid image of inadequacy in the short story "White Nights: A Sentimental Love Story from the Memoirs of a Dreamer." The protagonist moves from day to day in a stale and unprofitable life that lacks intimacy with another individual. He is lonely and feels the loneliness deeply. All that begins to change one night on a bridge near his home. He encounters a woman who is crying. Concern for her wells up within him, a depth of concern that is unfamiliar to him. Speaking to her out of his concern results in such a powerful sense of intimacy that he asks her to return the following night. "I can't help coming here tomorrow. I am a dreamer. I know so little of real life that I just can't help reliving such moments as these in my dreams, for such moments are something I have very rarely experienced."[1] His inadequacy in personal relationships is deeply felt, and he now experiences an opportunity to turn that around.

1. Dostoyevsky, *Best Short Stories*, 11.

A Month of Prayer and Gratitude

Occasionally, many who pray experience an inadequacy—an inadequacy of words, an inadequacy of expression of a deep longing or need. In those moments, this teaching from the book of Romans offers the assistance of the Spirit. When words fail us, the Spirit is sufficient to overcome our difficulty. John Calvin, a leading church leader in the 1500s, beautifully notes, "We are supplied with heavenly assistance and strength."[2] Simply, the promise here is that we are not left alone in our stumbling for adequate words. We are transported to Dostoyevsky's bridge, where we meet the Spirit who speaks to God on our behalf. We knock on God's door in prayer, and God responds with an impulse of the heart that we are understood even in the absence of words. As the protagonist in Dostoyevsky's story, we also experience a powerful sense of intimacy—an intimacy with God through the intercession of the Spirit.

It is the ultimate paradox—where we are the weakest, God's power is the strongest. We are unable to pray as God would have us pray. The Holy Spirit searches our hearts and crafts prayers on our behalf. It is, finally, an act of grace. Where we are inadequate, God completes the work of prayer. It is work because it results in changes in attitudes and behavior—changes that are the direct outcome of prayer. It is sacred work because it results in a conversion from seeking God's blessings for our own small projects to becoming captivated by God's hopes and dreams for us. The Spirit's prayer on our behalf results in an interruption of our lives. We become attached more firmly to God's redemptive work in the world. Looking back on the shape and character of our former prayers, we realize how inadequate they really were. They were about us, not about God. They were about our individual pursuits, not about a life in a relationship with God.

What remains is a promise. When we don't know how to pray, when we are at a loss to communicate effectively with our Lord, the Spirit restores communication. From the earliest pages of the Bible, we see that human rebellion and sin broke intimacy with God. That resulted in our hiding from God when God came walking in our

---

2. Calvin, *Commentary on Romans*, 198.

garden. With "unexpressed groans" the Spirit pleads our case before God. We know that God is receptive to the prayers of the Spirit on our behalf because the Spirit "pleads for the saints, consistent with God's will" (Romans 8:27b). Now we have confidence in our relationship with God—and for our future—because both are now held in God's grasp, not ours. Without the Spirit interceding on our behalf, it is a certainty that we would continue stumbling in sin and hiding from God. Because God has now taken control of our feeble utterances, we can now rest quietly before God, confident that the Spirit will express well our longings.

God of grace and mercy, thank you for the available power and presence of the Holy Spirit, my abiding Comforter, who helps me pray in moments too deep for my words. Dear God, you understand my most traumatic wounds. They shout for attention and try to upstage your Spirit's balm in me. May the Holy Spirit pray through me today and pray me through these moments as I struggle today in prayer. Help me to let go and allow your river of living, abiding water to flow through my weakness and my human inadequacy. I surrender, Lord, and I rest in the joy of your precious and holy gift. In the name of Christ, I pray. Amen.

25

It's Still Life

SUSAN SPARKS

> *Give thanks to the Lord, because he is good; because his love endures forever.* —1 Chronicles 16:34

Recently, I saw an image on social media that said "Life*" at the top, then underneath, in small print by the asterisk, it said: "Available for a limited time only, limit one per customer, subject to change without notice, provided 'as is' without any warranties, your mileage may vary." While this was meant as something to make people laugh, it packed a powerful message. Amazingly, we tend to believe that life comes with some type of warranty that promises things will always be easy, fun, and painless. And when it's not, we complain—incessantly.

We complain about the weather: "Oh my goodness, it's so cold, when will it ever stop?" Then, two months later we carp: "Oh my goodness, it's so hot and humid, when will it ever stop?" We whine that the trains and buses are late. We moan that people are rude, the stock market hasn't done well, or that the grocery store is out of our favorite item. Recently, I was at Whole Foods, and I heard a woman complaining to the manager that they were out of her "soy milk substitute." First, what is soy milk substitute?

And second, why would anyone want it? We waste so much time complaining about the superficial things that we miss precious seconds, hours, days, even years of our life. It's like the Jewish prayer: "Days pass and years vanish, and we walk sightless among miracles."[1] We must be grateful in the good times and the bad, for in the end, it's still life.

Warnings like "life is short" get greeted by eye rolls and shrugs. Yes, we've all heard this saying many times—which is part of the problem. We have heard it so much that we have become immune to it. But there is urgency in those three short words. Things can change in the blink of an eye. We don't know what is going to happen from one day to the next. We don't know if we will be given tomorrow—or even the rest of today. Just look at the headlines: random shootings, tornados that tear apart entire towns, and soaring cancer statistics. Life—is—short. It is also sacred. The psalmists offered this wisdom: "You are the one who created my innermost parts: you knit me together while I was still in my mother's womb. . . . I was marvelously set apart" (Psalm 139:13–14b). Life is the greatest, most sacred gift we have. Sure, you may think other things are important, but if you didn't wake up this morning, then what difference would it make?

Life is short. Life is sacred. And because of that, it should be celebrated in the good times and the bad. It doesn't matter where you find yourself: a long line at the Department of Motor Vehicles, the dentist chair, or the chemo room, it's still life and there is joy to be found in the simple taking of a breath. The author Elisabeth Kübler-Ross wrote, "People are like stained-glass windows. They sparkle and shine when the sun is out, but when the darkness sets in, their true beauty is revealed only if there is a light from within."[2] Find that light. Strive to be grateful in all circumstances. Use that gratitude to inspire and lift up others who are mired in difficulty. We were never guaranteed that life would be easy, or fun, or painless. Yet, even in the pain we can be

---

1. Quoted in Hughes, "New Year's Prayer," para. 4.
2. Clemmer, *Leader's Digest*, 84.

grateful for the simple gift of being alive, because in the end it's still sacred, it's still a gift, it's still life.

Loving Giver of Life, today I need a perspective adjustment, not only to see you more clearly but also to live more courageously with a spirit of holy expectation. After all, Lord, this sacred life I have is a precious gift to be cherished, to be enjoyed, and to be nourished in all its sometimes scariness. I confess, merciful Savior, that I do not give myself ample rhythms of intentional gratefulness as I make my way through each day. Today I will begin by celebrating your goodness in the quietness of this moment of prayer. I give you back today the gift of my life for you to do something beautiful with it. I will go out with you to inspire someone before this day is over. Jesus, in your gracious name, I pray. Amen.

26

Quiet, Lonely Places

NATHANAEL HOOD

> *News of him spread even more and huge crowds gathered to listen and to be healed from their illnesses. But Jesus would withdraw to deserted places for prayer.*—Luke 5:15–16

Scattered throughout every hospital, there are nooks and crannies, closets and pantries known only to those who work there: an empty room in an otherwise overcrowded wing; a secluded walk-in between units; a lonesome hallway tucked away in a corner few visit since the last round of renovations. In these places the hustle and bustle of medicine—the loud shrieking of machines, the pungent odors of sickness and bodily waste, the panicked cries for help—fade away until everything is still and quiet and peaceful. Look into any of them and you might find an exhausted nurse taking a catnap, a stressed doctor checking their phone, or a resident standing in the corner, eyes closed, brow furrowed, fists clenched as they collect themselves with deep, slow, steady breaths. And sometimes, if you're lucky, you might find a hospital chaplain.

Having worked as a hospital chaplain for over a year now, I can confidently say that few hospital employees know these secret places better than we do. Unlike most doctors and nurses who largely stick to their assigned floors or units, we chaplains are expected to respond to crises and consultations throughout the entire building, and we do—I suspect only the security guards and custodians have the lay of the land quite like us. And considering the work we chaplains do, finding these hidden places where we can rest and recenter ourselves is nothing less than a matter of survival. More than once, I've left the side of families grieving the unexpected loss of a parent or child after crying, praying, and sitting with them for hours only to glance at my phone and see my shift isn't even a quarter over yet. I've worked overnights where I've been called to gunshot wounds and stabbings at two in the morning. And I've literally been bedside and watched patients die with my own two eyes while their loved ones wailed into my arms. Doctors, medics, and surgeons are able to emotionally distance themselves from these situations, but the opposite is expected of us chaplains—our domain is that of misery, pain, grief, and tragedy.

Some might be surprised to learn that our supervisors actually encourage us chaplains to take multiple breaks in these quiet areas throughout our work day. After all, we live in a culture that idolizes overwork and exhaustion. Too often we treat those who work eighty-plus-hour weeks with admiration and not horror. Missing important life events—childbirths, birthdays, funerals, family gatherings—for the sake of our employer's bottom lines isn't just commonplace; it's often expected. Ask any clergyperson and they'll tell you some of the most frequent regrets shared by widows and widowers was that they worked too hard and didn't take that vacation they'd always wanted, they kept putting off that special trip they'd planned together, they forgot to *live* with their partners while they still had life left to live with them.

In seeking these daily moments of solitude, we chaplains—at least those of us who identify as Christian—reflect none other than the life and ministry of Jesus himself. Again and again, in the Gospels, Jesus is hounded by boisterous crowds looking for healing and guidance. Remember, one time, a crowd literally tore the roof off the house where Jesus was staying so he could heal someone! But over and over, the Gospels also show Jesus slipping away from the crowds to "deserted places" where he could be by himself and pray. Jesus understood that solitude with God wasn't just important; it was necessary for him to do the work he needed to do. I wonder what our world would look like if more people prioritized solitude and silence in their private and spiritual lives. Perhaps we as a nation would be less stressed, less tired, less anxious. It's worth a try. The wonderful thing about solitude with God is you can literally start practicing it at any time. All you need is the will to try and a quiet, lonely place that only you can find.

God of rest and sweet peace, my burdened, stressed, and overworked soul thanks you for the gift of sanctuary spaces. Help me to intentionally resort to these secluded nooks and crannies of quiet, to which I can escape and be re-created in the loving embrace of your strong and everlasting arms. Blessed Savior of Sabbath rest, designed for human restoration, I exhale and thank you for these blessed spaces of seclusion. Give me the desire each day to consciously seek out an inner shelter for my often unrested body. In remembrance of Jesus, my perfect example of rest, I pray. Amen.

27

Conditions of Answered Prayers
Doug Hood

> *If you remain in me and my words remain in you, ask for whatever you want and it will be done for you.* —John 15:7

Ernest Hemingway captures the deep disquiet among many who are faithful in the practice of prayer, Christians who go to their knees in prayer but quietly question just how much they can expect from God. Distressed by doubts, a lack of confidence in God's ability—or desire—to respond to prayer plagues their practice of prayer. In his short story "The Gambler, the Nun, and the Radio," Sister Cecilia expresses her heartfelt desire to be a saint—a faithful, sincere desire that she has carried since she was a little girl. Sister Cecilia was absolutely convinced that if she renounced the world and went into the convent, she would become a saint. Now, years later, she still waits for her prayer to be fulfilled. Mr. Frazer, the protagonist of the story, responds to her, "You'll be one. Everybody gets what they want. That's what they always tell me." But Sister Cecilia expresses doubt, "Now it seems almost impossible."[1]

The great nineteenth-century preacher Phillips Brooks once addressed this common difficulty so many people have with

---

1. Hemingway, "Gambler," 382.

prayer—explaining that the Gospel of John identifies two qualities shared by those who can hope to pray successfully. First, what does it mean to "remain in me"?[2] It is a phrase that is familiar in the New Testament. To offer clarity, Brooks asks that we think of a child in their earliest years. Those are the years children are so completely absorbed or "hidden" in their parents' life that you do not look upon them as a separate individual. They are expressions of their parents' nature. The child's thoughts and speech are nearly echoes of the parent. In these earliest years, we hear a child utter something, and immediately we know what has been spoken by the parents in earshot of the child. The parent acts and thinks for the child; the child acts and thinks as the parent. Similarly, we "remain" in Christ as we grow closer to Christlikeness.

The second condition of successful prayer is in the words "and my words remain in you." This is the continual and instinctive reference of the definite, explicit teachings and commands of Christ, asserts Brooks. This second condition is not separable from the first—the first is remaining in Christ. In Christ, it is impossible to do anything, say anything, or desire anything but just what is the Lord's will. Yet, that is incomplete, imperfect, and unreliable without some positive and definite announcement of it in our own words. Returning to the image of the child, words spoken are but echoes of what is heard. To "remain" in Christ necessarily produces the thoughts and words of Christ—a striving to full obedience to the teachings of Christ. Brooks eloquently puts it this way: the soul remaining in Christ makes ready to accept Jesus' words, and then the words lead into a deeper utterance of the desires of God's heart.

Returning to Hemingway's short story, Sister Cecilia's prayer for much of her life was that she might become a saint. Discouraged that the prayer remains unanswered, she concludes that it may be an impossible prayer. Readers of this short story identify with her—we also have prayers that seem to remain unanswered year after year. How do we reconcile unanswered prayer with the promise that whatever we ask will be done? Perhaps the difficulty is that we jumped with hearts so eager to receive that we failed

---

2. Brooks, "Prayer," 297.

to notice the prior conditions here in John's Gospel. Ultimately, prayer is about one thing—joining our lives so completely with Christ's that Christ's life and ministry continue through us. Prayer is a commitment to reverse the departure of our lives from the life and purposes of Jesus. As we strive to return our lives back to Christ and to "remain" there and have Christ's words remain in us, our prayers take on fresh power.

Blessed God, help me to draw closer to you in this moment of heartfelt prayer as I seek to grow in greater alignment with your life in me. I confess my tendency to doubt your goodness and to drift away from you in thoughts, words, and deeds. You are the joy of my life, and my heart's deepest desire is to remain ever so close to you and your living Word, which is the source of my strength, power, and perseverance. Merciful God, deep in my heart, I believe you will give me the best and most loving answers I seek. I wait with eyes and heart wide open in the assurance of your goodness. In the name of Jesus my Christ. Amen.

28

Wheat and Weeds

MICHAEL B. BROWN

> *Two men looked out from prison bars. One saw the mud. The other saw stars.* —Dale Carnegie[1]

We've all been told time and time again that life is 10 percent circumstance and 90 percent perspective. I'm not sure the stats are that dramatic, but it's probably close. We hear it all the time: "It is what it is." Life happens. It's how we interpret it that makes the difference between happiness and hopelessness.

Jesus told a fascinating parable about how we see things (Matthew 23:24–43). The owner of a field and one of his chief servants were standing side by side looking through the same window at the same plot of ground. The servant was alarmed, pointing out that an enemy of the farmer had come and sown weeds in the wheat field. There were weeds were everywhere. Might as well just set fire to the whole acreage. The owner, however, replied that if his servant would take a closer look, he would also see wheat growing in the field alongside the weeds. His advice was to wait till the day of harvest, gather the wheat, and then burn the weeds. One saw a

---

1. Carnegie, *How to Stop Worrying*, 135.

disaster. The other saw a harvest. *Two men looked out from prison bars. One saw the mud. The other, stars.*

I once asked Fred Craddock what gift he would give to each of his children if he could give them only one. He immediately replied: "That's easy. I would give them the gift of a grateful heart because that will determine how they experience everything else in life." There are weeds in every field, if that's where we decide to focus.

No person is perfect. You may recall the story of a husband and wife driving home from church one Sunday. The minister had preached on "Be ye perfect, even as God is perfect." The husband said to his wife: "I wonder how many perfect people there actually are in the world." She answered: "One less than you think!" No person is perfect, but they (we) always exist alongside the assurance of grace.

No job is perfect. There will be bumps and bruises, but they always exist alongside the reality of senses of accomplishment, purpose, fulfillment, and personal pride.

No marriage is perfect. But husbands and wives always exist alongside the vows "to love and to cherish" even in spite of the weeds of "in sickness and in health, for richer or poorer."

No church is perfect, but every church exists alongside the biblical truth that "we have this treasure in clay pots" (2 Corinthians 4:7), and though imperfect, they are still holy. In every church I've ever served there were saints—not sinless people, but good and decent and faithful people who made the world a better place.

We could go on and on with this, but you get the point. Life happens. It's how we interpret it that makes the difference between happiness and hopelessness. Craddock was right—a grateful heart will determine how we experience everything else in life.

I often encourage people to create a thanksgiving journal. That's simply a book or notepad that you put next to your bed. Every night before the lights are turned off, write down one good thing you experienced or witnessed that day. Admittedly, it may have been a long, tiring, or difficult day. Even so, there is always at least one blessing we can recall. Write it down. Then write down another the next night and another the next. On the final night of every month, read aloud the entries from your journal. Doing so will remind us that when we pay attention, we will always discover blessings. In time, that practice will create within us spirits of gratitude, which will determine how we experience life itself. It will help us, in spite of the weeds, to see the wheat and celebrate it.

Dear God, give me eyes wide open to look around and see imperfect, earthly saints like me striving to live with gratitude for your abundant goodness toward us all. Your blessings and love are new every day. I sometimes walk past them in my urgency to get through another day, and I miss expressions of your love and human beauty. Slow me down, Lord. I need to pay attention and take time to deepen my perspective that life is more than breathing. I commit my life today to grow spiritually in more intentional ways. I will use a journal resource as an aid to my spiritual growth. May this dialogue with you, this inner conversation with the Spirit, this deep listening give me insights as I write, paint, or draw. I open my mind for wisdom to interpret the thoughts and blessings you will give me. I accept this blessing with a grateful heart. Amen.

29

God's Treasures

GRACE CAMERON HOOD

> *You are precious in my eyes, you are honored, and I love you.*—Isaiah 43:4a

The Holly House is a ministry of First Presbyterian Church of Delray Beach. Women get together each week to change the world. They make incredible crafts, do service projects, socialize, eat together, and enjoy one another. They have formed a support system based on fun, faith, and creativity. Everyone is welcomed and included. They are a microcosm of what the church strives to be.

Each year, Holly House participates in a time-honored and universal ministry of churches everywhere. They sponsor a rummage sale. The proceeds of the sale go to the ministry of the church. This is how it works. If you have something that you do not need or want or can't use anymore, you donate it to the church. The women sort everything. This is a time-consuming and tedious job. Imagine sorting hundreds of donated shirts according to size and price. When the sale happens, the community come in droves. Someone might see an item and realize that they want it, they need it, or they have a use for it. They pay for it. This is a wonderful system. What becomes one person's discard, trash, or burden becomes the next person's treasure. This is recycling at its very best!

What does this have to do with a book on gratitude? One day, I was looking through a table of delicate china teacups at the Holly House that had been donated. I grew up with those multicolor aluminum tumblers (which are now collector's items), white mismatched mugs, and "unbreakable" Corelle cups. I love china teacups. As I studied the intricate and colorful teacups, I was overwhelmed with a feeling of gratitude for what I have. I am grateful for many things. I inherited a lovely set of teacups decorated with beautiful violets from my grandmother. They are gorgeous. What's more, I have the entire set, which includes plates, serving bowls, miniature salt and pepper shakers, a matching sugar and creamer set, and, finally, small ashtrays for the bridge games my grandmother would host. What I have is more than I wanted. It is more than I thought I needed.

My gratitude goes beyond what I have. It speaks to who our God is. God wants us to have more than we can imagine. What God gives us may not be riches or things. God offers us a sense of worth that comes from who God says we are. We are not unwanted, unneeded, or a burden. I am grateful that with God, we are each precious and valued. That is one important thing to remember about God. All of us are wanted and loved. There is no one on earth whom God discards, donates, or sells. We are not a burden that is carried around or hidden away in an attic or basement when interest has died. None of us is chosen as second best. We all have immense value in God's eyes. We are all precious and a treasure to God. There is more. When we look at people around us, we need to remember that God values them! We need to treat people around us as if they were precious to God. This changes how we look at the world. As we see the world through the eyes of gratitude, our perspective changes and creates the community that God intended. One of love, acceptance, inclusivity, and care.

God of infinite resources, we give thanks for your many treasures and blessings in generous display all around us. You are always close to us in the beauty of your love, and may our gratitude always point to you and infuse us with boldness to display your grace to this world. We are thankful for the opportunity to celebrate the various support ministries of this church, a spiritual charging station. Today, we joyfully remember the fun and Spirit-inspired creativity of the Holly House and its dedicated volunteers. They make us all look good. They allow your light to shine brilliantly in this church and in the wider community. Thank you for their special events like the glorious mundanity of rummage sales and their exemplary display of stewardship with our resources. They inspire us to do something brave and new with our lives. They remind us, blessed God, that there are more important things in life than our possessions. Your generosity and love are the ingredients that give us and all we possess value, and that all people everywhere are precious and valuable to you. Continue to challenge us, Lord, to serve in the loving ways of your Son, Jesus the Christ. In his name, we make this prayer. Amen.

30

Two Little Words

NATHANAEL HOOD

> *This, then, is how you should pray: "Our Father in heaven, hallowed be your name . . ."*—Matthew 6:9 NIV

Of all the teachers I had while studying for ministry at Princeton Theological Seminary, few left as remarkable an impact on me as C. Clifton Black, the Otto A. Piper Professor of Biblical Theology. As the author of over twenty books and more than two hundred published articles, he was an academic institution unto himself, a one-man library of biblical insight. Lover of jazz, Shakespeare, classic Hollywood movies, and impeccably tailored three-piece suits (regardless of the weather), he cut the impression of a man who drank deeply and joyously from the well of life. His immensity of character spilled into the classroom where, frequently overcome by emotion, he would punctuate important points by slamming down an open palm and bellowing like a Baptist preacher. He did just that during my first class with him in a course examining Jesus' parables. "*Every word,*" his hand pounded on the table one early spring afternoon, "of Scripture is *pregnant* with meaning!"

This first lesson has stayed with me over the years since my graduation. When we read Scripture too quickly or casually, we risk missing important details that could otherwise transform our understanding of God's holy word. Consider, for example, the Lord's Prayer. As presented in the Gospel of Matthew, the prayer is taught by Jesus as the model for how all Christians should pray. But for many Christians, the prayer is less a matter of devotion than one of muscle memory, a word or phrase repeated over and over again until it loses its meaning. But in his masterful commentary on the Lord's Prayer, Dr. Black forces readers to slam on the brakes and consider each word with the same care we would use to view a precious jewel. What, Dr. Black asks, is the prayer actually saying to us?

Remarkably, much of the answer can be found in the prayer's first two words: "Our Father." *Our* father. Not *my* father, not *your* father, not *his* or *her* or *their* father, but *our* father. The first word of the first line is an invitation to community. "The Lord's Prayer is never privatist," Dr. Black writes, "[The word 'our'] pulls the Prayer's supplicants out of selfish individualism into a relationship of ever-expanding generosity."[1] Of course, this isn't to say that we can't or shouldn't pray specifically for ourselves and our own needs—Jesus himself prayed for his own deliverance from the cross in Gethsemane. But in this first word of the Lord's Prayer, Jesus presents us with a model of community.

And what is that model? That can be found in the second word: our *Father*. Not *Leader*, not *Lord*. Not *Creator* nor *King*, not *Liege* nor *Ruler*. We come to our God as little beloved children, not cowering subjects. Put together, the two little words "our Father" are not just an address but a command. Remember, they whisper, that even in our solitude, each of us is part and parcel of a sacred community held together by a mighty God, a Lord who protects and cherishes each of us as equals. Yes, it is good and proper to pray for our own needs. But here in the Lord's Prayer, we hear Jesus slam his own hand on the classroom table, reminding us

---

1. Black, *Lord's Prayer*, 78.

that true prayer should be the antidote to selfishness. True prayer should lead to selflessness instead.

O God, true and heartfelt prayers sometimes sneak up on us, and prayer becomes our teacher. Prayer teaches the open heart. Prayer teaches the heart to love. Prayer leads us into new perspectives, new pathways, new ways to see the loving and often-broken heart of God. Teach my heart, holy God, to learn the joy of selflessness today. Open my eyes to see people as Jesus saw them, as people in need: people who needed to be loved, people who needed to free themselves from living intolerant lives, people who needed to climb over cultural and gender barriers, people who needed to see the tender heart of his Father, our Father, my Father, God of us all. Hallowed be your name. Amen.

31

Beyond the Fence

Greg Rapier

> *Jesus did many other things as well. If all of them were recorded, I imagine the world itself wouldn't have enough room for the scrolls that would be written.* —John 21:25

In elementary school, I had a friend named Clay who bragged that he had the best backyard in the world. He claimed to have two basketball courts, a soccer field, and a playground—all in his backyard. One day, Clay invited me to his house. We walked there after school, and I remember, upon entering, racing toward his backyard.

I rushed outside, looked around, and felt incredibly disappointed. A couple of trees, a barbecue, a football... but not much else. The whole yard was smaller than one basketball court—let alone two. Let alone a soccer field. And a playground? Forget about it.

I told Clay his backyard wasn't big. And it wasn't special.

Clay calmly picked his football off the grass and chucked it over the fence. Then he began to climb. "Come on," he said. But I was afraid. I'd never climbed a fence before, and I was scared. Slowly, I began to climb. Just a step or two, enough to peek over the top. And sure enough, next to his football, on the opposite side of the fence, there were two basketball courts, a soccer field, and a playground.

Turns out Clay shared a fence with our elementary school. And that great big backyard that he often spoke of was right there all along.

John 21:25 reminds us that the Bible—for all its value and beauty—is a limited tool and that the verses of Scripture can't possibly capture the totality of who God is. This verse, the final one of John's Gospel, doesn't seal God's story shut but rather allows it to unfurl, to open up and bloom like a flower. It reminds us that God is alive and vibrant, even outside of Scripture. It invites us to see past the fences we construct—the fence of church, the fence of Scripture, the fence of scarcity and limited resources—to see past the small-minded lies we tell ourselves about a limited God in a scarce and Godless world, and to imagine a God of abundance. The Scripture calls us to get rid of a boxed-in God and, instead, step across the fence into God's great big backyard, an open space full of wonder, mystery, and abundance, where God's story is still being written today. And where every new discovery is a reason for gratitude.

Blessed Emmanuel, God of unlimited power, of infinite and beauteous things, of the micro and the macro, you go with me wherever I go, and you are present in all my daily encounters. You fill this vast universe, yet your most loved place is the intimate sanctuary of the human heart. Help me to dust off all the limitations I place on you, all the tiny boxes I place you in, all the exaggeration of knowledge I claim to have of you, all the people I keep you from. Open my heart to embrace your inexhaustible and unbounded love for me, and for this distracted and fallen world. Your love mixed with your amazing grace outstrips all my wrongdoings. I live in the freedom of discovering unlimited possibilities and in the gratitude of knowing that the eternal God lives with me. In Jesus' name. Amen.

An Attitude of Gratitude

MICHAEL B. BROWN

Jesus told them another parable: "The kingdom of heaven is like someone who planted good seed in his field. While people were sleeping, an enemy came and planted weeds among the wheat and went away. When the stalks sprouted and bore grain, then the weeds also appeared. The servants of the landowner came and said to him, 'Master, didn't you plant good seed in your field? Then how is it that it has weeds?' 'An enemy has done this,' he answered. The servants said to him, 'Do you want us to go and gather them?' But the landowner said, 'No, because if you gather the weeds, you'll pull up the wheat along with them. Let both grow side by side until the harvest. And at harvest time I'll say to the harvesters, "First gather the weeds and tie them together in bundles to be burned. But bring the wheat into my barn."'"
—Matthew 13:24–30

Brothers and sisters, we ask you to respect those who are working with you, leading you, and instructing *you. Think of them highly with love because of their work. Live in peace with each other. Brothers and sisters, we urge you to warn those who are disorderly. Comfort the discouraged. Help the weak. Be patient with everyone. Make sure no one repays a wrong with a wrong, but always pursue the good for each other and everyone else. Rejoice always. Pray continually. Give thanks in every situation because this is God's will for you in Christ Jesus.* —1 Thessalonians 5:12–18

A grandma told me recently about an experience she had had last Christmas. Her six-year-old grandson, a first-grader, was all excited about the annual February Broadway Bash at his elementary school. A whole afternoon was set aside for every first- and second-grade class in the school to present musical skits. It was a big deal for them. The other grades got to come watch, and, of course, all the parents and grandparents were invited. All autumn, my friend's grandson talked about that upcoming event. The little girls were told to wear a dress for the program. And the little boys were told to wear a white shirt with a tie.

Well, my friend said she had decided to become part of what her grandson was so excited about. She would buy him his first tie. So, she shopped and shopped because any old tie would not do. Finally, she found the perfect one. On Christmas morning, he unwrapped the box and found it. His very first tie. On Christmas morning . . . for a six-year old . . . a necktie. I gotta tell you, I'm a lot older than six, and even I wouldn't be too excited about receiving a necktie for Christmas. Well, he put it down and tore into the other boxes. A bit later, his grandmother saw the little boy dutifully approaching her with the tie in his hands. Now, what I love about this is the grown-up language he used. He reached his grandmother, held the tie out in front of him, and said, "Mom said I need to thank you for this. I assume there must be a reason." Is that great or what? What six-year-old phrases things that way? "I assume there must be a reason."

Yes, there was a reason. His mom had planted a seed that when it becomes a full-grown flower can affect his life about as much as anything else at all. I was at a retreat with the late Fred Craddock years ago. One night in an address Craddock made to us, he said, "The queen of the spiritual virtues is a grateful heart because it determines how we see life and how we understand God."[1]

Jesus told a story about that very thing. In Matthew's Gospel we read of two men standing before the same window, looking out at the same piece of land. The men are a landowner and his chief steward. The steward is frustrated to the core, disappointed, and almost devastated by what he sees. "Look at your field, which was sown with wheat," he says. "Some enemy has come and sown weeds. Now, all I can see is a field full of weeds. Do you want me to burn it down? Maybe you can file an insurance claim and get a few dollars back. It's just a disaster!" But the owner of the field—mind you, looking out the same window and at the same crops—answers, "No. Because, in addition to the weeds, I also see a field of wheat. Let them grow alongside each other until the day of harvest. Then you can burn the weeds, but sell the wheat" (paraphrase of Matthew 13:24–30).

That parable is about us, about our lives in our world. In every field there, wheat grows alongside weeds. This is not Shangri-la. We're not in heaven. Yet. Ours is not a perfect world, nor has it ever been, nor shall it ever be in mortal time. That does not mean that we resign ourselves to suffering, of course. Paul was very clear about that in the passage from Thessalonians. We are to do everything we possibly can to help those who hurt—the hungry, the homeless, the displaced and dispossessed, the lonely or left out or left behind, the abused or abandoned: "Live in peace with each other," he wrote. "Comfort the disheartened. Help the weak. Be patient with everyone" (1 Thessalonians 5:14–15). We do all that we can as often as we can. But, at some point, we understand that we cannot fix all

---

1. Graham, "Four Roads to Meaning," s.v. road 4, "Spiritual."

broken things all the time. And so, thinking about Christ's parable, the difference for us much of the time between a life of frustration and a life of fulfillment is a matter of focus. As Craddock put it, to focus on that for which we can be grateful will determine how we experience life and how we interpret God.

1. *An attitude of gratitude* is not necessarily something with which we are born. Instead, it's something we develop, a spiritual discipline like all the other spiritual disciplines. It is something we long for and work toward.

I enjoy going to the gym three or four times a week . . . for about one month a year. That's usually in January. After a month, I'm done with it and long to return to buffets and no treadmills. This past year, I did not go in January because I had gone in September, and those two months were just too close together. Anyway, one day back in September, I was standing in a short line waiting for one of the weight machines to come open. Standing beside me were two guys who looked like young versions of Arnold Schwarzenegger. They had muscles popping out of their muscles. They were discussing their exercise routines. One of them said, "Do you have any idea across the years how much weight lifting and how many workouts it has taken to get a body like this?" I thought that was a tad vain, so (since I was standing right beside them anyway) I injected myself into their conversation. I shouldn't have. I wasn't invited. I just couldn't help myself. When he said, "Do you have any idea across the years how much weight lifting and how many workouts it has taken to get a body like this?" I said, "Do you have any idea across the years how much pasta and pastries it has taken to get a body like this?" I laughed. Apparently, their sense of humor had not developed as much as their biceps.

It's the same with our souls. We become what we choose to develop. We are what we think. We can focus on spiritual disciplines or emotional junk food, on wheat or weeds. Paul understood when he wrote to the people in Thessalonica that maintaining a positive focus about life is not always easy. Those people were being buffeted on each side. On the one hand, there were Pharisaical zealots who opposed them. On the other was

Rome and its maniacal Caesar Nero. There were a lot of weeds in their garden. Paul understood that. But, he said to them, in that very kind of a world, a world where you suffer and struggle, "Give thanks in every situation because this is God's will for you in Christ Jesus" (1 Thessalonians 5:18). This is what will spell the difference between frustration and fulfillment. This is what will keep the boat afloat in troubled waters. You can't always change the world, Paul was saying, but if you can change the way you see the world, you can survive. It's not always what's in your field. Instead, often, it's what's in your heart.

I heard the late Charles Stanley remark once that choosing to be thankful (and thankfulness is a choice) is like driving in your car and changing the station on the radio from music that annoys to music that soothes.[2] He was right. It's a choice we get to make. It's a choice we have to make.

My wife and I were at a Christmas party last December. While there I met a man confined to a wheelchair. He is a retired educator who lived a successful, productive, active, and very healthy life. Only recently has his health changed. He said to me: "I could let this chair hold me down. But instead," he continued with a sweep of his arm pointing at the people in the room, "I let these friends lift me up." He made a conscious choice to be grateful. It's a discipline to develop a worldview in the field of our lives that makes the difference between frustration and fulfillment.

2. *An attitude of gratitude* is transformational. As Paul understood, and as we understand, we can't always fix a broken world. We do what we can where we can when we can. But we cannot always fix everything. However, we can change the way we look at life, and in time that changes us.

I was in a conversation some time ago with a woman who told me about going through a season of depression. It wasn't chemical. Instead, it was environmental. She had been hit by a tidal wave of things coming in rapid succession: the loss of a friend, the loss of a job, the loss of a relationship, a temporary financial setback, one thing after another after another until she

---

2. Stanley, *Grateful Hearts*, 37.

was broken down and beaten up by life. Every day felt dark, and gloomy, and frightening. Someone encouraged her to begin journaling, which she did. Each night, she would write down a litany of her thoughts and experiences. "If I didn't feel bad enough already," she told me, "that made everything infinitely worse. Because every page was filled with the trials and tragedies of my life. I told my friend about that, and she advised that every night, I should include in my journaling one good thing I had seen or experienced that day. So, I tried again. Sometimes 'one good thing' didn't seem all that easy to come up with, but I did. And when I wrote it down, I would take a highlighter and color that one good thing. Periodically, I would read back through my journal, but only the highlighted part. Eventually," she told me, "I came to realize that the counselor helped me find insight, the medication helped me find sleep, but it was the journal that helped me find hope. Things turned around for me when I figured out that every day of my life, God sends something good to highlight."

You remember the old hymn "Count Your Blessings": "Count your many blessings, name them one by one; / Count your many blessings; see what God hath done."[3]

It is medicinal to do that. Transformational. *An attitude of gratitude* heals our hurting spirits and gives us hope by remembering that every day, God sends something good to highlight.

3. Finally, *an attitude of gratitude* is an act of praise. That's what Paul told the Thessalonians. "Give thanks in every situation because this is God's will for you in Christ Jesus" (1 Thessalonians 5:18). This, he was saying, is how you will find God and how you will understand Christ Jesus, when you look at the highlighted parts of your life.

Years ago my wife and I accompanied a group from our church on a trip to South Africa. I was the pastor of Marble Collegiate Church in New York City at the time. Our mission ministry included a number of schools, orphanages, and homeless shelters in the poorest parts of that country. One Sunday morning, I preached at a church on the edge of Botshabelo. At that point

---

3. Oatman, "Count Your Blessings," refrain.

in time, life for most people there ranged from one of poverty to one of abject poverty. There was a 70-percent unemployment rate. About a thousand people a day died of AIDS, not because there was no medicine available but rather because they had no money with which to buy the medicine. Whole families lived in little metal huts that looked like the sheds where many of us keep our lawn mowers. Entire communities were served by a single well where people walked a mile a day to draw a bucket of water and a mile back to take it home.

Sunday morning came, and the people arrived at their beautiful little white-framed church. The parking lot had four or five cars at most because they didn't own cars. They walked.

Many wore sandals. Some came with bare feet. Most walked several miles to reach the church. But they kept coming and coming until it was full to capacity. They wore their Sunday best. Men were in suits. Women were in white dresses with large hats. Some had owned those outfits for decades, but they wore them only on Sundays. And they kept them mended, and clean, and starched to honor God.

When the church was full, the service began. "We don't worship by a clock," the pastor told me. There was a lot of music, a lot of prayer, and a lot of fellowship. Finally, it came time for me to preach. The pastor stood nearby, interpreting my words for his people. After the sermon came the offertory. It was a moment I will never forget, an experience beautifully etched into my memory. One of the elderly church mothers came forward. She was barefoot, wearing a beautiful white dress and a large hat. A table had been set up in front of the chancel. On it was a wicker basket to receive the gifts of the worshipers. The church mother called for the offering, encouraging people to come forward and bring their symbols of thanks to God's church. They immediately began their procession to the table. They began at the back of the sanctuary and made their way down the center aisle. Row by row, they came. A few held cash. Most had a few coins. For many, it was a sacrifice to find a single coin at all, but they did. As they came forward, the choir began to sing a rhythmic, uplifting song. It is how they came that I will never forget. The very old, the very young, and all those in between did not walk down the center aisle. They danced. They danced with coins in their hands and arms uplifted, swinging and swaying on bare feet, twirling with broad smiles on their faces, all the way to the table, then around the table before dropping their coins in the basket. Then they danced back to their seats, still swinging and swaying, smiling and singing with the choir. They offered a down-deep-from-the-heart litany of praise for the gifts God had given. Most of them had precious little so far as material possessions were concerned.

I remember thinking that I have so much they will never possess. But they've got something that I need. In spite of their existential circumstances, they danced to the altar in gratitude because they knew that God loved them and was with them and had given them a new day, and friends, and family, and church. There were more weeds in their garden than most of us can begin to imagine. But they were able to see and celebrate the wheat.

In truth, we have so much, don't we? So many lines of life are highlighted in yellow. The loves we have, the friends we have, the families we have (or those who are like family to us), the churches we have, whatever measure of health we have, the faith we have, the life we have, the God we have who offers us grace and goodness, fresh starts and second chances, abundant life in this world and eternal life in the world to come. Knowing that, how can we keep from dancing?

"I have said these things to you so that my joy will be in you," said Jesus, "and your joy will be complete" (John 15:11). He didn't speak those words in a perfect, pain-free moment. Rather, he spoke them in the upper room only hours before being crucified. In a broken, imperfect world, he came that we might find a spirit the world cannot take away, a spirit of joy. So, how do we find that? Paul said this is how. "Give thanks in every situation because this is God's will for you in Christ Jesus" (1 Thessalonians 5:18). A grateful heart is the queen of the virtues because it determines how we see life, how we interpret God, and eventually, it makes us want to dance.

Am I Gonna Ride This Thing or Not?

SUSAN SPARKS

> *In those days Caesar Augustus declared that everyone throughout the empire should be enrolled in the tax lists. This first enrollment occurred when Quirinius governed Syria. Everyone went to their own cities to be enrolled. Since Joseph belonged to David's house and family line, he went up from the city of Nazareth in Galilee to David's city, called Bethlehem, in Judea. He went to be enrolled together with Mary, who was promised to him in marriage and who was pregnant. While they were there, the time came for Mary to have her baby. She gave birth to her firstborn child, a son, wrapped him snugly, and laid him in a manger, because there was no place for them in the guestroom.* —Luke 2:1–7

Today, we listened to two of the great Christmas Scriptures: the story of the wise men and the story of Mary and Joseph heading to Bethlehem. As beautiful as they are, ironically, these are also the two Scriptures that have caused me—as a minister and as a human being—the most confusion.

Sparks—Am I Gonna Ride This Thing or Not?

Take the story of the wise men coming to pay honor to the baby Jesus. Every year I read that story, I have the same question: Why would you bring frankincense? Yes, I know it was an expensive and sought-after perfume and all that. And maybe they gave it thinking it would be like an air freshener for the manger? However, if you were going to visit a young couple who had no home, no money, and a new baby, would you not maybe bring . . . diapers? Or a baby monitor? Or some organic carrot and mango baby food pouches? But frankincense?

This brings me to our second Scripture, the one that raises a question with which I have struggled my entire adult life. Let me set the stage for that Scripture.

First-century Nazareth. We are sitting in a little stone house with Mary and Joseph. Mary is eight months and twenty-nine and a half days pregnant, and Joseph has just told her that she has to travel—by donkey—ninety miles from their home in Nazareth (basically at sea level) up a three-thousand-foot mountain range where Bethlehem sits in order to—wait for it—answer questions for a census guy.

I know this is the holy Mother Mary and all, but that conversation could *not* have been pretty. Let's just say that Mary was most likely not singing the Magnificat.

While the book of Luke doesn't tell us this specifically, my best guess at what happened after Joseph's shocking announcement is this: Mary stares at Joseph, then turns, looks out at the poor little donkey chomping on his breakfast, and thinks to herself, "Am I gonna ride this thing or not?" In short, do I have a choice?

Tell me that's not a scenario we can all understand. We all have those moments when we are confronted with a huge, scary difficulty in life, and we ask ourselves: Am I gonna ride this thing or not? In short, do I have a choice in this situation?

Sometimes, we have a clear choice, which makes the answer easy. Like, for example, am I going to swerve through three lanes of traffic, risking my life and everyone around me, because I just saw the hot sign come on at Krispy Kreme?

While it's tempting to say yes, the answer is "No, I'm not riding this."

Or should I spend my entire day scrolling online through newscasts, Facebook posts, Instagram images, and TikTok videos about a baby hedgehog?

Answer: "No, I'm not riding this."

Or here's a good one: Do I need to respond to that person who has done something or said something that made me really mad?

Answer: "No, I'm not riding this."

And let me just offer this little aside: not everything requires our response. There's a great old saying: "Just because someone spews out trash doesn't mean we are in the business of digging through the garbage."

A few weeks ago, there was a video that went viral about a woman in Ohio who got mad about something with her order at Chipotle. I watched the video. It was astounding. The woman was screaming at the young cashier, and when the manager stepped in to defuse the situation, the woman took her food and flung it in the manager's face.

But there was a happy ending to all this. The woman was arrested, and the judge sentenced her to jail or to work in a fast-food restaurant for two months.

Amen?!

Friends, we have a choice in *if* and how we respond to other people. You want to create a little *peace* in your life? Wait it out. Take a breath. And just say, "No, I'm not riding this."

But then, in life, sometimes the answer is not so easy. Sometimes we are faced with things completely out of our control.

- Do I have to ride this cancer diagnosis?

    Answer: "Yes, I gotta ride this."

- Do I have to ride this depression I'm in?

    Answer: "Yes, I gotta ride this."

Sparks—Am I Gonna Ride This Thing or Not?

- Do I have to ride this job loss—this financial pressure?
  Answer: "Yes, I gotta ride this."

- Do I have to ride this chronic pain?
  Answer: "Yes, I gotta ride this."

- Do I have to ride this addiction that's tearing my family apart?
  Answer: "Yes, I gotta ride this."

And it was the exact same analysis for Mary.

- Do I have to ride this donkey ninety miles up a three-thousand-foot mountain?
  Answer: "Yes, I gotta to ride this."

It's in those situations where we have very little control—when we have almost *no* choice but to get on that thing and ride it—that we must look to Mary to see how she got through.

While the book of Luke does not specifically share what she did, common sense would tell us that in order to ride that donkey up that mountain, Mary had to do two things. First, get as much padding as possible.

Maybe Mary had Joseph shear a bunch of sheep and make a soft, fluffy pillow on which she could ride, or maybe she just loaded a bunch of blankets over the poor little donkey. In fact, perhaps we should stop for a brief moment of silence for the donkey. [Silence observed.]

Now, back to Mary. If she was gonna ride that thing, she needed as much padding as possible. And so do we! Like Mary's, maybe ours is a literal blanket. Who doesn't love a good blanket? But maybe we should also consider some more creative options. For example, one of the best sources of padding is cultivating a sense of gratitude.

Gratitude makes for some great padding. We tend to take so many things for granted. We focus on what's missing in our lives as opposed to the blessings right in front of us.

A Month of Prayer and Gratitude

Last year, I was speaking in a fancy town on the Connecticut coast. The morning of the event, I went to a local coffee shop and found myself in line behind two wealthy matrons in head-to-toe resort wear. This was the conversation (spoken in a Connecticut lockjaw accent):

First woman: "You must be looking forward to your upcoming trip to Paris!"

Second woman: (big sigh) "I am looking forward to Givenchy, but I've seen Versailles, and how many times can you do the Louvre?"

We tend to focus on what's missing in our lives. Honestly, what do we really need beyond food, water, clothing, and shelter? And please understand that by food, water, clothing, and shelter, I don't mean truffles, Perrier, Prada, and a McMansion. You can *also* live well with Ruffles, Pepsi, Payless, and a motor home.

Somebody gimme an amen!

Friends, we must be grateful for what we have. Even in the worst of circumstances, we can always find something—one thing—that is going right. Even in the worst of circumstances, we can find something that is healing. Even in the worst of circumstances, we can find something, even if it's something tiny, that brings us joy.

Whatever it is, find it. Be grateful for it. And remember the words of the great philosopher and Holocaust survivor Victor Frankl: "Everything can be taken from a man but one thing . . . to choose one's attitude in any given set of circumstances."[1]

Gratitude can change your attitude. It can keep your eye on what's important. Think about Mary. As she rode that donkey up that mountain, in the midst of her pain, her sights were on Bethlehem and her goal: to give birth to a Messiah.

So, Mary rode that donkey ninety miles up a three-thousand-foot mountain. Step by difficult step.

This makes me think of my dear friend Dr. Otis Moss, senior pastor of Trinity Church in Chicago, who once gave a sermon on Psalm 23. In it, he said that he believed the most important word in

---

1. Frankl, *Man's Search for Meaning*, 75.

Sparks—Am I Gonna Ride This Thing or Not?

Psalm 23 is "walk." I think Dr. Moss is absolutely right. Think about it. The psalmist didn't say, "Yea, though I sit in the shadow of the valley of death" or "Yea, though I am stuck in the valley of death."

No, the psalmist used the Hebrew word *halakha*, which means to go, walk, or travel. When we focus on the word "walk" in Psalm 23, we realize that any time we find ourselves in the shadow of the valley of death or the shadow of a huge obstacle or the shadow of change and transition, the best and only thing we can do is, like Mary, keep our eyes on Bethlehem and just keep walking.

So, first you get yourself some padding of gratitude and perspective. Then, like Mary, you must do a second thing: pray like crazy.

I'm not Catholic, but perhaps that ride up to Bethlehem is where the rosary started. For every step that donkey took, Mary was probably counting the hairs on its neck, praying each time, "Have mercy."

Sometimes we may feel that way, too, especially during those hard times in our lives when every step in the ride is difficult, when every step—we pray—is the last. Or those times when we reach the point where we think we can't go one step farther.

I'm sure Mary felt that. But you know, you just know, that she also prayed—really hard. Why? Because, like good padding, prayer is about gratitude. It empowers us to transcend our own human weaknesses and access a power beyond us.

When we pray, every angel in heaven comes flying to our aid. Guaranteed. No qualifiers, no exceptions, no exclusions. And you can trust me on this because I'm a lawyer.

Friends, there are things in this life over which we have no control, things that we're just gonna have to get on and ride, but there is a silver lining to all this. Even riding through the hardest of times, remember that if we're riding, we're climbing.

Every step that donkey takes, every day you get through, is a step closer to Bethlehem. And the more padding and prayer you give yourself, the easier the ride. But there's one more lesson, and this is perhaps the most important lesson of all: you never know what can come out of a difficult ride. At the end of her ride, Mary gave birth to a Messiah.

So, this morning, let me ask you this: What things can you bring forth from your pain that are redemptive and healing?

I wish each and every one of you a beautiful, peaceful, and joyful new year. But if peace and joy aren't possible in your life right now, that's okay. Just remember that whatever you're going through, God is going through it with you. There's only one question left that you have to answer: Am I gonna ride this thing or not?

FOMO

Thomas K. Tewell

> *When you pray, don't be like hypocrites. They love to pray standing in the synagogues and on the street corners so that people will see them. I assure you, that's the only reward they'll get. But when you pray, go to your room, shut the door, and pray to your Father who is present in that secret place. Your Father who sees what you do in secret will reward you.'*
> —Matthew 6:5–6

> *Ask, and you will receive. Search, and you will find. Knock, and the door will be opened to you. For everyone who asks, receives. Whoever seeks, finds. And to everyone who knocks, the door is opened. Who among you will give your children a stone when they ask for bread? Or give them a snake when they ask for fish? If you who are evil know how to give good gifts to your children, how much more will your heavenly Father give good things to those who ask him.*—Matthew 7:7–11

I love the story of the five-year-old boy whose parents were having a dinner party one evening. He was on summer vacation, and he was just underfoot. He was so in his mother and father's way that everything they did to get ready for the dinner party, the boy undid within a few seconds. The last straw was when his mother came down from getting dressed, and she looked at the dining room table, which she had set so beautifully with gorgeous flowers and all the appointments. But when she looked at that dining room table, she saw, to her horror, that the boy had eaten all of the cherries off of all of the fruit salads. That did it! The mother was livid! She grabbed a newspaper, wadded it up, and started to chase the boy around the house to give him a good whack with it! But he bounded around the house and went down the front steps and got on his hands and knees and crawled under the front porch, and he hid way in the back of the porch. The mother was about to get on her hands and knees and chase after him, but just then, the father drove in from doing a few last-minute errands, and the mother was mad and said, "Do you know what this son of yours has done? He's eaten all the cherries! I want you to crawl under that porch, and I want you to punish him, do you hear me!" The mother stomped up the steps and into the house. The father got down on his hands and crawled over toward the little boy, and as he crawled over to where his son was, he saw his two eyes way in the back under the porch, and as he crawled over nearer and nearer, he heard his little son say, "Is she after you too?"

The good news of the gospel is that God is after us . . . but God is not after us to punish us, or to harm us, or to hurt us. The reason God is on his hands and knees is that God wants to find us in the hiding places of our lives and call us out of the darkness and into God's marvelous light, so we are free to live and love as God meant us to live and love. And the reason God chases after us is that God is desperate for a relationship with you and with me.

There is an acronym in our culture today that describes the nature of God. We may not see it at first, but I believe it describes the nature of God. It's the acronym FOMO, "fear of missing out." So often, young people in our culture have an appendage attached to their body, and it's their mobile phone. And any time a tweet or a text comes in, or an email or anything comes in on social media, they can't let it alone for even a second or two. They are constantly on their phone looking at it because they have a fear of missing out on this text or this tweet or whatever is going on. Now, here's the surprising news of this text for this morning, which is what Jesus is saying to us. God has FOMO. God has a fear of missing out . . . on us! God doesn't want to miss anything going on in our lives. If we're worried about something, or anxious about something, or afraid of something, God wants to know about it. God already knows about it, but God wants us to tell God about it. And if there's a challenge or a joy or something that we're ecstatic about, or we have hopes or dreams or aspirations, God wants to know about all those things too!

God does not want us to miss his wisdom, his discernment, his guidance for our lives. God sees so many people in our society who run away from God and hide under the porch, and God comes chasing after us to guide us out of the darkness of ignorance into God's marvelous light of the knowledge of God. And God has given us an amazing vehicle to stay in touch with God every single day of our life. Do you know what that vehicle is? Prayer. Prayer is a gift from God so we may communicate with God and so that God may communicate with us. This morning on this communion Sunday, there are three important things God wants to teach us about prayer. I hope you will write these on the screen saver of your mind so that you can always call them up whenever you need them.

The first thing God wants to teach us about prayer is that prayer is an intimate conversation with God. In Palestine, when Jesus lived, the Jews took prayer very seriously. They wanted to pray every hour of the day and night, rain or shine, but there were several times a day that they appointed for prayer. The day began at six o'clock in the morning, so they set aside the third hour, nine o'clock; the sixth hour, twelve noon; the ninth hour, three o'clock; to truly focus on God. And wherever you were at the third, sixth, or the ninth hour, you should stop and pray to God. But what if you're in the marketplace, or right by the synagogue, or in a busy neighborhood street, what do you do then? Jesus said, "Don't be like hypocrites" (Matthew 6:5a), from the Greek word *hypokritos*, which means "actor." The actors in the plays would hold up a mask in front of them so you couldn't see their face, in other words if you were wearing a mask, you were not being your authentic self. So, he said, beware of the *hypokritos*, those who wear a mask, because they're only acting like they're praying. They like to pray in the synagogue or on the street corner and the busy marketplace. They like to have everybody around when they pray, and then they raise their hands to God and they shout to God, and they may be right in the middle of the marketplace, and when they do that people might say, "Oh, that Doug Hood, isn't he religious? Isn't he righteous? Isn't he holy?" But, Jesus said if you do that you already have your reward. What I want you to do is go into your closet and pray to God in secret, so your prayer is intimate conversation with God. God wants you to tell God the desires of your heart. God wants you to be totally honest with God. What's your motivation for prayer? Is it to call attention to yourself and have people say, "Oh, you're so wonderful," or is it to be in contact with God? Prayer is a vehicle to be in communion, in contact, with the Living God of the universe. Here's the other thing, it's not that public prayer is bad. People might say, "Well then, we should never pray in public, we should never pray in a group." No, it's the motive of prayer that is the key. Is your motive so the people say, "Oh, you are so great!" or is your motive to commune with the Living God? Prayer is communication with God.

  The second thing God wants to teach us about prayer is that prayer is not to change God's mind but to receive God's mind. Very important. Jesus teaches us that if we who are evil know how to give good gifts to our children, how much more will our Father in heaven want to give good gifts to God's children, to all of us? He says this remarkable thing, "Ask and it will be given to you; seek, and you will find; knock, and it will be opened to you" (Matthew 7:7–8 KJV). That's a remarkable statement, for everyone who asks receives. Everyone who seeks finds. To everyone who knocks, the door will be open. Now, does that mean God always gives us what we want? No! I hate to say that. See, the purpose of prayer isn't to change God's mind as if we must wrangle out of God some good gift. Jesus says God is more eager to give you good gifts than you are even to receive them. But, the purpose of prayer is to get to know God, not to change God's mind, to give us good things—God's inclined to give us good things—but the key to prayer is receiving God's mind, receiving what God wants to do. So, what do we get when we pray? Now listen carefully: when we pray, we will get what we asked for, we will get what we are seeking, we will get what we are hoping to get because the thing we want to get when we pray . . . is God.

Let me illustrate. Some years ago, Suzanne and I were at Princeton Seminary with two of our dearest friends, Gary and Sara. They had a little boy the same age as our little boy Ryan, and they grew up together. They then went on to Texas and we went on to New Jersey to churches, and we heard that Corey, our friend's son, had a rare form of leukemia. Gary and Sara were in Texas, so they took Corey to the hospitals in Austin, Texas, and then they took him to MD Anderson Cancer Center in Houston, and then they went to Switzerland to a famous medical center there. All the while, they and we were all praying that Corey would be healed. We prayed in New Jersey, they prayed in Texas, congregations in California prayed, and congregations in Alabama prayed for Corey, but Corey didn't get any better. And then came the day when Corey died. Now, people all over the world were praying for Corey, so what did they get for all their prayers? Did Corey feel better? No. Was he healed physically? No. Did he come back to life after he died? No. No, no, no . . . they didn't get what they wanted . . . but what they got was the thing we always get when we pray. They got *God*! A God to give them the stamina to face the death of their son. A God to give them perseverance to keep on keepin' on amid the challenges and vicissitudes of life. They didn't want Corey to die, but God gave them the stamina to go on. And God gave them the hope that someday they will see their son alive again in the kingdom of heaven, and they believe that. So, what they realized is the resurrection is God's ultimate healing. See, they didn't get God to change God's mind. Actually . . . they got to receive God's mind, and they realized God loved them and Corey more than they loved themselves. Prayer is a mystery; it isn't just to get what we want; prayer is to receive the mind of God. Prayer is not a problem to be solved, but it's a mystery to be wondered.

Unless I miss my guess, there's somebody here in this congregation today or watching a streaming video who is angry at God. Unless I miss my guess, there's somebody here who's prayed and prayed and prayed for something . . . college acceptance; prayed and prayed and prayed for an illness to be cured; prayed and prayed and prayed not to get a divorce, that a marriage would work together; prayed and prayed and prayed for something and God didn't seem to give you what you want. But in this text, "Ask, and you will receive. Search, and you will find. Knock and the door will be opened to you," the tense of the verb is an aorist tense, a continuation tense, in other words—keep on asking, keep on seeking, keep on knocking and the door will be open to you. Maybe not the door you want, but the doorway to God. I say this very tenderly to some who are in the midst of some real challenges: prayer is a mystery. God does not always give us what we want, but as we keep on praying, keep on seeking, keep on knocking, we find God more faithful, we find God more loving, and we find that God gives us more strength than we ever thought was possible. Prayer is not to change God's mind; God is a good God, he wants to give us the desires of our heart, but we live in a world filled with vicissitudes, and challenges, and illness, and cancer, and leukemia like Corey died of, and actually God can operate through all these things to give us something greater than even physical healing, to give us faith to endure when all else fails. I say it so tenderly to you . . . but we tend to run away from God and crawl under the porch and never want to see God again. But, if we can just stick with God and keep praying and keep seeking and keep knocking, the door to God will always be open. I know that's tough to hear but ultimately is the only thing that brings us comfort.

The third thing God us wants to know about prayer is that God is desperate to hear from us. In fact, God is so desperate to hear from us that God will get on God's hands and knees and crawl over to us and seek us to call us out of the darkness into the marvelous light. In a moment when the elders and the deacons come to your pew to serve you communion, they're going to come right to your pew, and they're going to hand you the elements. When they do, I want you to picture Jesus Christ coming right to you and remembering you and calling you by your name and say, "Valerie, and Doug, and Kim, and Stacey, and Miller—I haven't forgotten about you, I came right to your pew today to say I'm with you in whatever it is you're facing." I want you to receive those elements remembering that God has brought them right to your pew. God is desperate to hear from you, and during that communion, when you're taking that bread and wine, I hope you will remember to talk to God honestly and openly about whatever is on your heart, and soul, and mind. God is desperate to hear from us.

Some years ago, our son, Ryan, became a plebe at the United States Naval Academy in Annapolis, Maryland. He was eighteen years old when he started Plebe Summer, and it wasn't easy. It was a six-week grueling time with the initiation into the Naval Academy rituals, and Suzanne and I and our other son, Toby, took Ryan to the Naval Academy. We flew from Texas, where we were living at that time, to Philadelphia and got a rental car and we drove over to the Naval Academy. We had a meal with him, and in the morning, he had to go into the Navy Yard, get his uniform, get his hair cut, and all that. And then we said goodbye to him, and we cried, and he got a tear in his eye. It wasn't easy to let him go. But we had planned a nice trip with Toby that we would go up through New England and to Boston and see some sights and then Toby would fly back to Texas for a basketball camp. Then, Suzanne and I would drive to North Carolina, where I was going to perform a wedding for the daughter of some of our dearest friends. We were going to go to that wedding and then stay through Sunday, and then we would drive leisurely from North Carolina back to Philadelphia 539 miles. But we had all day Monday to do it, it was an evening flight back to Texas... so it was easy to do.

So, the Friday when we got to the Naval Academy and dropped Ryan off, the superintendent said, "In nine days, a week from Sunday, between eleven a.m. and one p.m., these plebes will be able to call home, so please be there to get their phone calls. They are going to be desperate to talk to you." But see, we had planned this vacation, and we were away at the wedding. And Sunday, we're going to see our friends in Charlotte and, then, Monday, drive leisurely to Philadelphia. But, this call would be Sunday morning, and we wouldn't be in Texas. This was before cell phones, so what do you do? We did the wedding, hugged the parents and the bride and groom, and we got a new flight out of Philadelphia at six-thirty a.m. on Sunday morning, and we drove all night 539 miles from Charlotte, North Carolina, to Philadelphia during the wee hours of the morning from eight p.m. to five a.m. in the morning. We handed in the rental car at the airport, got on the plane, and landed in Houston. Somebody picked us up and we got home at a quarter to eleven. Ryan was supposed to call between eleven a.m. and one p.m. So, I went out to get some breakfast for Suzanne and me. I got home—we were sitting by the phone eating our breakfast and, at about eleven-thirty a.m., the phone rings. Now we were prepared for the worst, we knew it was going to be terrible—Plebe Summer is not easy, it's particularly hard. The first six weeks are grueling, and we thought he was going to say, "I want to quit the navy, I don't like the navy, I hate the naval academy," we were prepared for the worst. And so, the phone rings, and Suzanne answers the phone, and she says, "Hi, Ryan, how are you?" and he says, "I'm fine, I'm great!" and I said, "For this, we drove all night!"

But we wouldn't have missed it. Do you want to know why? Because this kid is our boy, this is our son, and we want to know his hopes, and dreams, and fears, and anxieties, and if he wanted to quit. We just wanted to hear about it; we just wanted to be a part of his life. So, if parents would drive 539 miles in the middle of the night to get to the airport and fly to Houston, Texas, to take a phone call with our son who says, "I'm fine," how much more does God want to hear from us?

I hope when you think about prayer, you don't think of it as some ethereal thing in the sky, in the clouds, way out there—somewhere. Think of it. It is right here, that God wants to know *us.* God has FOMO, a fear of missing out on you and me! And God doesn't want to miss us, and once we understand that truth, we understand that prayer is about connecting with God! Jesus doesn't want any of us to miss God . . . do you?

Secret of Contentment

Bruce Main

> *I know the experience of being in need and of having more than enough; I have learned the secret to being content in any and every circumstance, whether full or hungry or whether having plenty or being poor.* —Philippians 4:12

Author A. J. Jacobs describes himself as "petty and annoyed." He's forgetful of the three hundred things that go right every day and focuses on the three things that go wrong. This self-avowed curmudgeon decides he wanted to become a better person—to learn to be more content and grateful. But how? He decides to take a "gratitude journey."

This gratitude journey began by thanking everyone involved in producing his morning cup of coffee. Everyone! You see, the act of noticing is the first act of gratitude.

So, Jacobs intentionally thanks the barista who rings him up at his local shop, finds the local guy who roasts the beans . . . and thanks him. He calls an artist in Seattle who designed the lid for his cup. Thank you! He tracks down truck drivers and warehouse workers, the people who pick the beans in Columbia, and the custom workers who guard the borders. Thank you! Thank you!

Of course, the workers are bewildered. They've never been thanked. Jacobs even drives out of New York City to the Catskill Mountains and thanks those who guard the watershed—99.9 percent of our coffee is water, after all. Every thank you on his journey turns into a story. New relationships are formed. A deeper appreciation is developed for each person's role in his coffee supply chain.

By the time Jacobs finishes his "gratitude tour," one thousand people have been thanked. Crazy to consider: a thousand people involved in creating his morning cup of coffee! In retrospect he finds himself embarrassed for complaining about paying $2.57 a cup. Practicing gratitude helps Jacobs become grateful.

Years before A. J. Jacobs ever thought about gratitude, the apostle Paul was eloquently suggesting that he had discovered a "secret"—a secret possessing the power to transform a life.

"I have learned the secret of being content in any and every situation," he wrote (Philippians 4:12 NIV). Scholars feel that Paul was borrowing language from the Greek mystery religions where a person needed to go through a series of challenges to "discover a secret." The implication is that contentment is a learned behavior. Discovering contentment is a challenge.

Some of us might react defensively to Paul's claim. "Wait a minute," we refute. "Paul doesn't know what's going on in my life. I'm suffering. He's an ivory-tower theologian who is detached from reality."

Not so. Paul writes these words from a Roman jail—a rather hideous place—waiting for possible execution on trumped-up charges. Prisons were literally holes in the ground where one's family had to provide food to keep one alive. No "three hots and a cot."

So, from this hellish place, Paul writes—to ordinary, working-class folk with no health care or 401(k)s—that he has learned an important *secret*: contentment. An audacious claim, isn't it? Paul challenges us to consider the truth. Contentment is a state of being independent from our possessions and circumstances.

Deep down, most of us know this to be true. We have met people living in bitter poverty . . . yet they are full of joy. We've known people who have suffered tremendously yet still choose to forgive and love. We know people who give the shirt off their back, because their needs are secondary to others. History is sprinkled with people who transcend their difficult circumstances. They have discovered the secret of contentment.

I remember Doris, who attended Logan Memorial Presbyterian Church. She was in her late seventies when we met. Her life hadn't been particularly easy. After losing her husband to cancer, Doris went back to work as a psychiatric nurse—while raising four teenage girls on her own. Despite her very real challenges, Doris always chose gratitude.

For years, Doris sent me a $30 gift every month to help our work with inner city youth in Camden, New Jersey. One day, I opened her envelope and a $15,000 check fell out. "Dear Reverend Main," she wrote. "I was going to purchase a new car but decided to send you the money to build your new high school." I was humbled and elated. Two weeks later, I received another letter from Doris. "Dear Reverend Main," she began. "Great news! I went to the doctor last week. He said I can't drive anymore. I didn't need my new car anyway!" What a great attitude. When Doris was diagnosed with cancer, she would always plan a lunch with a friend or a trip to the movies. *After* her treatment. "Why should going to the doctor be drudgery," she shared with me. "Now I can look forward to those visits!" When her eldest daughter had the sensitive conversation about what she wanted to have happen to her body after she died, Doris said with a smile and a wink, "I always wanted to go to medical school!"

But I'll never forget her memorial service when the pastor, Reverend Don Painter, gave an inspiring eulogy in her honor. "Doris was the most 'pro-choice' person I ever met," he exhorted. Then he clarified. "Not in the political sense. But she always chose joy and gratitude." I believe Doris had discovered the secret of contentment. It's possible.

Henri Nouwen, the late Catholic theologian, said, "Gratitude never comes without effort. The more we choose gratitude in the ordinary places of our day, the easier it becomes."[1]

Why is the apostle Paul so passionate about people learning the secret of contentment? I really believe that content people are liberated to serve more freely. Content people are other centered—interested and aware of other people's stories and lives. Show me a truly content person, and I'll show you a joyful person. The saints of Christianity reveal to us that joy is never found with the accumulation of stuff or the consolidation of power. The saints of the Christian faith show us that joy and peace can be found in the most difficult of human circumstances. Contentment is an inner state of being.

I know I have work to do in this area of my life. My trivial complaints are an indictment of my supposed spiritual maturity. At times I have the audacity to complain when my candied yams are too sweet and my vente triple-shot latte with cinnamon sprinkles is too hot. Oh my! And churches can be even worse. I hear complaints about the wrong font size in the bulletin, or the color of the pastor's tie, or the fact that bagels have been served for the past three weeks in coffee hour. Come on, saints! It's time we do some self-reflection and start discovering *what it can mean to be content in every and any situation.*

P.S. After the service at Delray Beach Presbyterian, one of the parishioners approached me. Sadly, I can't remember her name. But she made a great point! She challenged me to clarify the difference between complacency and contentment. She's right. Contentment is not complacency. Contentment doesn't mean to do nothing. Contentment, I believe, creates a kind of freedom and mental space that allows us to make a difference in the world. The apostle Paul was never complacent. He wrote letters to churches, preached sermons, and mentored leaders—even amid persecution and personal adversity. Paul's contentment provided a unique internal condition that allowed him to continue acting in ways that furthered God's work and witness in the world.

1. Nouwen, *Prodigal Son*, 85–86.

Gratitude

Hannah Anglemyer

> *I'm not saying this because I need anything, for I have learned how to be content in any circumstance. I know the experience of being in need and of having more than enough; I have learned the secret to being content in any and every circumstance, whether full or hungry or whether having plenty or being poor. I can endure all these things through the power of the one who gives me strength.* —Philippians 4:11–13

My math teacher from my freshman year of high school had a tradition each year right before we took midterms. She went around to each one of her classes with a little black bag containing a bunch of tiny rocks with motivational sayings or phrases etched into the front. Then, without knowing what the rocks said, we all reached inside and grabbed one. According to her, the rock you grabbed was supposed to be something you needed or something that could motivate you to get through midterms. The rock I grabbed had the word "gratitude" etched into its front. And so, taking its advice, I thanked my teacher for the gift and tucked it into a tiny pocket of my backpack I almost never touched. See, when I reach into my backpack, I'm usually looking for something—my trigonometry notes, my calculator, my Chinese textbook—or because I have midterms, tests, and then finals to worry about. But now, I'm a sophomore, and that's all still true! But my homework takes longer, my tests are harder, and for the first time ever, math doesn't make as much sense anymore. So I forgot about that little rock.

That was until a couple of weeks ago when I happened to reach into that same forgotten pocket and found that little rock right where I had first left it, the word "gratitude" still etched into its front. At first, I smiled at the memory and my teacher's kind gesture. Then I started to think. In the little over a year since I had first placed the rock in my backpack, I had become incredibly consumed by the homework I still needed to do, the test grades I didn't yet know, and with my math grade—which is lower than I would like. Finding the rock reminded me that even in the tiny world of high school, I still have so much to be grateful for. Though my math grade may not be what I want, it has improved from where it was! My teacher has gone out of her way to meet with me on several occasions to help me better understand the material, and every academic challenge I've faced has helped me to develop better study and time management habits. But it's easy to forget about gratitude when you're charging ahead to what comes next. It's difficult to pause and be grateful for what's in front of you right now.

I've found that applies outside of school too. When I was younger, my family and I would spend a large portion of the summer with my grandparents in the North Carolina mountains. One of our favorite activities was going on long walks or hikes together. Whenever we set out, I was always very eager for the adventures that lay ahead, oftentimes volunteering to wear a very stylish fanny pack, even when the length of a hike really didn't necessitate it. But, my attitude usually changed around halfway in. I would start to complain that I was tired of walking and could think of nothing but getting back home to a yummy snack and my favorite kids' show. My grandfather, "Doc-Doc," usually had other ideas, and he always seemed to find ways to add to the length of a hike, never missing a teachable moment. He would often pause to ask what felt like ten million questions: "So, Hannah, what type of plant is this?" or "So, Hannah, can you name that mountain?" As expected for a kid my age, I almost never answered correctly, which meant an even longer conversation involving a history or science lesson. Despite being moments I now look back on fondly, my eagerness to get back home prevented me from appreciating this time with family and the incredible beauty of God's creation surrounding me. Looking ahead to what could come next prevented me from being content with the blessings right in front of me.

In his Epistle to the Philippians, Paul writes that he has learned "the secret to being content in any and every circumstance, whether full or hungry or whether having plenty or being poor." It sounds like an incredible secret; after all, it's not easy to be content with the present when you don't know what the future holds. But Paul gives away the secret in the next line. He says he is able to "endure all these things through the power of the one who gives [him] strength." When we struggle to take moments to show gratitude or find ourselves ignoring what we already have, Paul teaches us to turn to God. Through God, we are able to find peace with what is in front of us now and give proper gratitude for all we have.

Bibliography

Bartlett, David L., and Barbara Brown Taylor, eds. *Feasting on the Word: Preaching the Revised Common Lectionary*. 12 vols. Louisville: Westminster John Knox, 2008–11.
Black, C. Clifton. *The Lord's Prayer*. Interpretation—Resources for the Use of Scripture in the Church. Louisville: Westminster John Knox, 2018.
Bonnell, John Sutherland. *No Escape from Life*. New York: Harper & Brothers, 1958.
Brooks, Phillips. "Prayer." In *"The Battle of Life" and Other Sermons*, 296–309. New York: Dutton, 1893.
Brueggemann, Walter. *First and Second Samuel*. Interpretation. Louisville: John Knox, 1990.
Buttrick, George A. *The Christian Fact and Modern Doubt*. New York: Scribner's Sons, 1935.
———. *Prayer*. New York: Cokesbury, 1942.
Calvin, John. *Commentary on Romans*. Edited by Timothy George. Theological Foundations. Nashville: B&H Academic, 2022.
Carnegie, Dale. *How to Stop Worrying and Start Living: Time-Tested Methods for Conquering Worry*. New York: Diamond Pocket, 2018.
Chevalier, Tracy. *Girl with a Pearl Earring*. New York: Penguin, 2000.
Clemmer, Jim. *The Leader's Digest: Timeless Principles for Team and Organization*. New York: TCG, 2003.
Cole, Allan Hugh, Jr. *The Life of Prayer: Mind, Body, and Soul*. Louisville: Westminster John Knox. 2009.
Dostoyevsky, Fyodor. *The Best Short Stories of Fyodor Dostoyevsky*. Translated by David Magarshack. London: Folio Society, 2021.
Fitzgerald, F. Scott. "The Offshore Pirate." In *Tales of the Jazz Age*, 70–96. Norwalk, CT: Easton, 1989.
Fosdick, Harry Emerson. *The Meaning of Prayer*. New York: Association, 1949.
Frank, Anne. *Anne Frank: The Diary of a Young Girl*. New York: Anchor, 2001.
Frankl, Viktor E. *Man's Search for Meaning*. Boston: Beacon, 1959.

BIBLIOGRAPHY

Graham, Ashton. "Four Roads to Meaning . . . and Here Is the Map." Ashton Graham, Mar. 2, 2024. https://ashtongraham.substack.com/p/four-roads-to-meaning.

Helsel, Philip Browning. *Pastoral Care and Counseling: An Introduction. Care for Stories, Systems, and Selves*. New York: Paulist, 2019.

Hemingway, Ernest. "The Gambler, the Nun, and the Radio." In *The Short Stories of Ernest Hemingway*, edited by Seán Hemingway, 353–91. Hemingway Library Collector's Edition 4. New York: Scribner, 2017.

Herbert, George. "Gratefulnesse." CCEL, 1633. From *The Temple*. https://www.ccel.org/h/herbert/temple/Gratefulnesse.html.

Hughes, Jurian. "A New Year's Prayer." Jurian Hughes, Jan. 10, 2022. https://jurianhughes.com/a-new-years-prayer/.

Kirkland, Bryant. "God's Gifts." *Princeton Seminary Bulletin* 7 (1986) 268–75.

Lawrence, Brother. *The Practice of the Presence of God*. Edited by Hal McElwaine Helms. Indiana: Paraclete, 1982.

Mays, James L. *Psalms*. Interpretation: A Bible Commentary for Teaching and Preaching. Louisville: John Knox, 1994.

Meyer, Joyce. "The Cause and Cure for Worry: Finding Peace in Trusting God." Joyce Meyer, n.d. https://www.joycemeyer.org/grow-your-faith/articles/the-cause-and-cure-for-worry.

Miller, Patricia. "Introduction." *Walking with the Father: Wisdom from Brother Lawrence*, by Brother Lawrence, edited by Patricia Miller, 7–11. Ijamsville, MD: Word Among Us, 1999.

Nightingale, Earl. *Successful Living in a Changing World*. Shippensburg, PA: Sound Wisdom, 2021.

Nouwen, Henry J. M. *The Return of the Prodigal Son: A Story of Homecoming*. New York: Doubleday, 1992.

Oatman, Johnson, Jr. "Count Your Blessings." Hymnary, 1897. https://hymnary.org/text/when_upon_lifes_billows_you_are_tempest.

Pinsker, Joe. "The Reason Many Ultrarich People Aren't Satisfied with Their Wealth." *Atlantic*, Dec. 4, 2018. https://www.theatlantic.com/family/archive/2018/12/rich-people-happy-money/577231/.

Presbyterian Church U.S.A. *The Presbyterian Hymnal: Hymns, Psalms, and Spiritual Songs*. Louisville: Westminster/John Knox, 1990.

Read, David H. C. *Preacher: David H. C. Read's Sermons at Madison Avenue Presbyterian Church*. Edited by John McTavish. Eugene, OR: Wipf & Stock, 2017.

Rohr, Richard. *Yes, and . . . : Daily Meditations*. Cincinnati: Franciscan, 1997.

Stanley, Charles. *Grateful Hearts*. Atlanta: In Touch Ministries, 2024.

Stewart, James S. *Walking with God*. Vancouver: Regent College Publishing, 1996.

Wood, Graeme. "The *Iliad* We've Lost." *Atlantic* (Nov. 2023) 81–92. https://www.theatlantic.com/magazine/archive/2023/11/emily-wilson-iliad-translation-homer/675444/.

www.ingramcontent.com/pod-product-compliance
Lightning Source LLC
Chambersburg PA
CBHW071212160426
43196CB00011B/2274